HOW TO TURN YOUR
SNAKES
INTO
LADDERS

HOW TO TURN YOUR
SNAKES
INTO
LADDERS

RUTH BENJAMIN

TARGUM/FELDHEIM

First published 1999
Copyright © 1999 by Ruth Benjamin
ISBN 1-56871-172-7

Published by:
Targum Press, Inc.
22700 W. Eleven Mile Rd.
Southfield, MI 48034
e-mail: targum@elronet.co.il
fax: 810-314-7550/toll-free fax: (888) 298-9992

Distributed by:
Feldheim Publishers
200 Airport Executive Park
Nanuet, NY 10954

Printed in Israel

TO
Rabbi Yisroel and Sara Feige Shusterman
and their family

And to my family
Uzi and Devorah Shinan and their family
Tzfon HaShamron, Israel

Yirmy, Rivky, and Esty van Halem
Brooklyn, New York

Yitzchok, Sara, Rikal, and Adina Levy
Brooklyn, New York

and to my late husband
Dr. Boroch Dovber Benjamin, *z"l*

הרב ישראל שוסטרמן

Rabbi Yisroel Shusterman

Modern society and technology is ever increasingly imposing upon humankind, leaving in their wake confusion and distortion of direction and purpose in life. Therefore, I was most pleased when Mrs. Benjamin mentioned to me that she was working on a book dealing with current issues facing modern psychology and Judaism.

Having known Ruth for the past twenty years, I have come to appreciate the many qualities of this very special lady. By profession, Ruth is a practicing senior clinical psychologist, with many years of experience, dealing with the broad range of human exposures and difficulties and, in particular, counseling those in need from within the Jewish community. As a mother, she has developed the necessary insights into raising children; as a friend, she has shown the true meaning of loyalty and concern, all carried out with great sensitivity and feeling.

Ruth maintains a very rigorous and disciplined personal daily schedule of *shiurim*, also attending public lectures on issues of *Yiddishkeit* and Jewish knowledge. She gives regular weekly *shiurim* to ladies, as well as being called upon to give guest lectures and talks relating to *Yiddishkeit* or women and family life from a Jewish perspective.

From all of the above she is most eminently qualified to put pen to paper and share her thoughts with the Jewish public. The popularity of her numerous previous books attests to Ruth's ability to communicate in the written form. I hope and pray that the world of Jewish readership will appreciate what Ruth has to offer in this book as well, to find help and support in their everyday experiences.

With Torah blessings for success in all matters, material and spiritual,

Rabbi Yisroel Shusterman

Department of Psychiatry

UNIVERSITY OF THE WITWATERSRAND, JOHANNESBURG

7 York Road, Parktown, 2193 South Africa • Telegram Uniwits • Telephone (011) 647-2026 • Fax (011) 617-2423

Ruth Benjamin is an experienced psychotherapist who is currently the senior psychologist at the Johannesburg Hospital and the University of the Witwatersrand. She trained originally as a social worker and later acquired a second qualification as a clinical psychologist. She is actively involved in both clinical practice and the training of psychology students. Her diversity of experience has allowed her to integrate a variety of psychotherapeutic approaches together with both her experience and religion to create a novel and practical approach to dealing with a wide range of life issues.

How to Turn Your Snakes into Ladders is a practical guide operating at many levels. Its aim is to give the reader both insights and tools to live life at a more optimal and fulfilling level. In this book, a method of going back into the past is used, a kind of "return trip," in which the person is encouraged to review a past situation and taught to apply new thought patterns derived from current maturity. This allows the past to be retrieved, edited, and refiled in a more healthy way.

This book contains the result of many years of accumulated experience and wisdom and covers a wide range of issues that many people will face. Topics covered include dealing with depression, anxiety, substance abuse, bereavement, stress, identity issues, disability, and relationships. This is a valuable and practical self-help resource that should assist people with a range of difficulties in a humorous yet insightful manner.

Michael Berk

Associate Professor
Department of Psychiatry

CONTENTS

*The snake was more subtle than all
the beasts of the field.*
— *Bereishis 3:1*

Introduction

SNAKES AND LADDERS

W hat's your favorite game? Monopoly? Scrabble? Trivial Pursuit? Well, for some of us it seems to be Snakes and Ladders. (Americans know this game as Chutes and Ladders.) We work hard to climb up the ladder of success, whether at work, with our family, or with our friends, but there always comes a point when we land on a snake and down we go.

We all have things that drag us down. We all have our own snakes. We might even recognize them, but we still find ourselves sliding down, down, down.

Here's one example of a snake whose tail often appears on the board toward the end of a game.

You have almost won. You're nearing the finish. And along comes a snake, and it whispers in your ear, "Who gave you the right to win? Have you led a faultless life? Are you a true tzaddik? Can you say you've never done any *aveiros* in your life? Look at the terrible things you've done! Not big things, true. But those little things... Remember?..." And you some-how find yourself declaring, "I am not allowed to be a winner."

Few of us are aware that we say this to ourselves. It might take some thought before we realize we're sabotaging our own success. Some of us always just miss getting to the top and attribute it to bad luck. It takes a lot of soul-searching to see how great a part we ourselves play in our failure. Some people spend years feeling they are being punished by Hashem while they are, in fact, punishing themselves.

We may blame others for our lack of success. We may blame circumstances. But often it is something inside us that holds us back.

If we could amplify the snake's whisper, we might hear him repeating words from the past:

"Your father always said you'd never make anything of yourself. And you won't."

"You've reached ninety-nine. Don't try for a hundred or you'll lose everything. Don't reach for too much."

"You know you hurt your sister, brother, aunt, uncle, wife, husband, father, mother, friend, neighbor. And they're still upset with you. How dare you succeed?"

"You cheated in ninth grade on that *Chumash* question, remember? Because of that you will never succeed, never reach the top."

The snake creeps into relationships, too. How many people break off something really special just before the other person is about to make a serious commitment?

A person may say to himself, *I broke it off because I knew she was going to break up with me soon anyway.* How-ever, deeper analysis will show that it was he himself who sabotaged his future happiness.

Many of us feel that we don't deserve to be happy, that we don't deserve to have someone love us. And we don't even realize we feel this way.

In this book we are going to identify some of these snakes. We will learn how to ignore their tempting words of destruction and even how to turn them into ladders. We will find ways to move up the board of life rather than down.

Because my patients trust me, I have not used exact case histories, though I have always drawn from true-life situations. I have tried to make people and places unrecognizable. The stories should be seen as illustrations to bring out a point.

I do not believe by any means that I have all the answers. In fact, I'm still discovering new ones every day.

Chapter 1

RETURN TRIPPING

How can we combat the evil snakes in our lives? How can we root out the old serpents that have coiled themselves firmly around our ankles? And how can we sidestep those waiting further down the road?

First we must identify the snakes in our lives. One important tool I use with my patients is called "return tripping." In return tripping a person goes back over past events, picturing in detail scenes from the past and reliving the feelings of key moments. After zeroing in on an emotionally loaded episode, the person is then able to bring in his adult knowledge and awareness and reevaluate what went on and what messages he has been carrying around in his subconscious ever since.

Thought and imagination can place a person in whatever time and location he chooses. If he so desires, then through thought and imagination he can place himself in the past of decades ago and experience it in his present time and location just as he experienced it then... And now that he is older and more experienced, with a certain lifetime behind him, he is able to view the same events more perceptively.

(Rabbi Yosef Yitzchak Schneerson,
the Lubavitcher Rebbe, 1934)

The mind has amazing powers to conjure up long-ago events.

Several years ago a young man named David came to see me. He had told me very briefly about a traumatic incident in his youth, and we decided to go into it in more depth.

David took himself back in time by picturing his childhood surroundings:

"I remember our garden. It was fairly well kept and had many flowers — roses and some tall orange flowers that looked like birds. There was a large jacaranda tree we used to climb and another smaller tree that kept its leaves even in winter..."

David had told me something terrible had happened in connection with his bicycle so I led him to that subject.

"DID YOU RIDE YOUR BIKE IN THAT GARDEN?"

David opened his eyes wide and started to cry.

"It was red and small. It had tiny wheels in the rear to stabilize the back wheel so I wouldn't fall off. I got it for my fifth birthday. It was shiny, with black rubber on the handlebars. The wheels were thick, with silver on the inside. It even had a little light on the front and a carrier in the back. I was so proud of it."

"TELL ME ABOUT YOUR FRIEND JOEY."

"He was four months older than I, and sometimes he would punch me, but I liked him."

"WHAT WAS HE WEARING THAT DAY?"

"I think he was wearing a red-checked shirt. Or maybe it became red afterward... I can't remember. He had red hair and freckles, and he seemed to be always sniffing."

"WHAT HAPPENED THAT DAY?"

"I didn't really want to lend him my bike, but I did. He got on it and went out the gate. I should have told him to stop, but I didn't. And suddenly there was a screech of brakes and a crash and an awful moaning, and then...silence."

"WHAT DID YOU THINK?"

"I thought, *My bike! My beautiful new bike!*"

"WHAT ABOUT JOEY?"

"I was sure he was dead, but I kept thinking about my bike." David was crying freely now. "I ran down and saw him. He looked so still and silent and sort of out of place where the truck had hit him. He was full of red, red blotches and lying in a pool of red, red blood."

"HOW DID YOU FEEL AFTERWARD?"

"Guilty. Terribly guilty. For years and years. It was my fault...like...I killed him..."

"DID YOU KILL HIM?"

"No, not really."

"THERE IS A CHILD INSIDE YOU, AND HIS NAME IS DAVID. HE CANNOT SLEEP AT NIGHT. HE KEEPS THINKING ABOUT THE ACCIDENT AND FEELING GUILTY. DO YOU THINK HE SHOULD FEEL GUILTY?"

"No."

"MAYBE YOU SHOULD TELL HIM THAT. IF YOU COULD GO TO HIM AND COMFORT HIM, WHAT WOULD YOU TELL HIM?"

"I would tell him there's nothing to feel guilty about. All he did was lend his friend his new bike. He did him a favor."

"WHAT WOULD YOU TELL DAVID IF HE SAID HE HAD KILLED HIS FRIEND? IS THERE ANY TRUTH TO THAT?"

"I would tell him that he is in no way responsible for Joey's death."

"TELL HIM THAT."

We got into our "time machine" and traveled straight back to that time. Because it was such a disturbing event, David needed someone to go with him.

This was one of the traumatic incidents which had caused David to feel he had no right to ever succeed. Every time he started to be successful in his job and a promotion was on the way, he would quit. He felt he did not deserve it.

In return tripping we can go to places in our minds, as David did, and replace our past understanding with our adult perspective. It involves an existential return to the situation and an attempt to change it.

Return tripping does not always come easily. Some people have a gift for visualization, and scenes of their past can be vividly described. For others the memory is more blurred.

Invariably, however, the person is able to picture far more than he ever imagined possible, and often other memories come crowding into his mind as well. Once he can visualize the setting of the scene, the physical surroundings, in detail, the emotions can be more easily recalled and situations can be relived with amazing clarity. People are able to see themselves as they were at the time, perhaps as children or teenagers — and they are able to talk to that child, or that teenager, explaining things to him, helping him and comforting him. A therapist can at times enter the situation together with the patient, to comfort or speak to the child, but primarily it is the person himself who must do the work.

When done properly, return tripping allows a person to heal his own soul as his psyche comes to terms with and alleviates the guilt and anger of past situations. This process may consist of numerous trips, either to the same event or to search out moments of bitterness and aggression from the earliest years up to the present.

The Method

On a practical level, return tripping can be done anywhere and at any time. However, it is better to do this with some kind of structure, perhaps at a certain time of day, in the same setting, in a favorite chair.

The person seats himself comfortably in a fairly relaxed position. He focuses his mind on an object from the past and describes it to himself or to whoever is with him — a toy, a picture, a cupboard, a clock. Inevitably, when the object is described, usually in great detail which surprises the one remembering, other memories start filtering through until the person has a picture in his mind of the room, the house, the garden. He can also choose to focus on a person, such as a teacher of a certain grade, a classmate, or a friend of a certain age.

As he pictures the scene from the past he remembers the people around him, his family and friends, and his enemies. He becomes sensitive to the atmosphere of that time.

Gradually he is able to focus on himself — the child — and ask, "What is the child feeling?" He is asking his present self what he thinks about the child's problem. He is, in fact, using his adult mind — his experience and his more mature intellectual and emotional functioning — to assess the situation at a distance. He then enters the situation and "talks" to the child, explaining it to him, often comforting him and "listening" to him.

If a person finds it difficult to talk directly to the child, he can view the child in the third person and speak to the therapist about him.

"WHAT DOES THE CHILD SAY?"
"He says his father's death is his fault."

"WHAT WOULD YOU SAY TO HIM?"
"I would tell him he is not to blame."

Doing a return trip once rarely works. For real results it is necessary to do many of these sessions. Early influences and experiences affect a child, and the adult has to go back at times to alter the effect. Sometimes, he has to alter attitudes he has picked up through the years which color his attitudes as an adult and can actually stifle his relationships with others, making him, in many ways, unable to respond correctly. It is important to trace the roots of our problems, to analyze them and work out ways of altering them and freeing ourselves from them.

Devorah was having trouble getting married. She would always be eager to meet someone and would enjoy the initial meetings, but as soon as the man showed real interest, she would switch off.

"TELL ME ABOUT THE HOUSE YOU LIVED IN."

Devorah described a stately manor with eight bedrooms, several servants, and an incredible coldness. Original pictures of well-known artists lined the walls and oriental carpets covered the floor. The smell of blossoms coming from the garden mixed with the smell of furniture polish. No dust could be found. I asked her to describe the curtains, which after a few seconds of thought she did. She began to remember the ornaments, the scratch on the table, the bowl which was always full of fruit.

She described the cupboard which she always had to slam shut so that everything did not slide out to preserve the elegance of the house. She never bothered to keep anything really tidy. Someone would always pick up her clothes and decide whether to wash them or hang them up. Someone would close the drawers she left open and make her bed.

She described the doll which always slept on her bed together with a fluffy blue cat she had gotten from an aunt for her birthday. One of the ears was torn, but she refused to part with him. She described her doll house. She described the dresses she had worn. She was, as it were, standing in the room.

"TELL ME ABOUT THE LITTLE GIRL WHO LIVED THERE. WERE YOU HAPPY THERE?"

"At times. When I was playing with my paint set."

"YOU WERE NOT SO HAPPY?"

For a minute Devorah looked like the child she was remembering as her face clouded over. "I spent many nights crying."

"WHY?"

"I don't know. There was nothing terrible happening. There was nothing happening at all. Until my...my...father just left..."

"TELL ME ABOUT YOUR PARENTS."

"As I said, my father left. I was nine. I saw him sometimes on weekends, but even before that he was a distant man. He would give me a peck on my forehead every night when he put me to bed and every morning before he went to work. I never saw him smile at my mother, nor did he shout at her.

"For a long time I felt this was the way he must be, and I drew away from the shadowy figure he was. I thought my mother was inherently right in everything she did.

"I can still see her there, telling me how men are only interested in taking advantage of women, that they are...awful. I still think they are awful."

As this was one of her problems, I wanted Devorah to stay in this scene and try to change it herself.

"HERE IS THIS LITTLE GIRL FEELING AWFUL WHEN SHE THINKS OF HER FATHER. WHAT WOULD YOU SAY TO HER?"

"I would tell her that maybe he isn't so awful."

"WHY?"

"Well, he provided well for my mother. He was clever. He worked hard. He never *did* anything awful."

"SO WHAT IS THIS AWFUL FEELING FROM?"

"Well, my mother said he was awful."

"WAS YOUR MOTHER ALWAYS RIGHT?"

"She also said I was awful, and that hurt terribly, but that was a different kind of awful."

I asked her to speak to the child and was amazed at the length and depth of her response.

"Devorah," she said, "Daddy wasn't awful. He left because Mummy called him those things, not because he didn't love you. Mummy didn't understand him, and she called him all sorts of things, but he never hurt you — he was never awful to you."

I knew healing was on the way, and after several more sessions of "seeing how the little girl felt," she was able to relate to men in a way that wasn't "awful."

Positive Return Tripping

It is sometimes necessary to go on positive return trips. Many people have the impression that delving into the past means concentrating on the negative and the traumatic. We tend to forget the healing power of bringing forth positive memories. We can go to many positive places in our minds.

Rabbi Abraham Twerski highlighted this point in one of his books. He cites the case of a man in his fifties who had undergone surgery for a recurrence of cancer and was in constant and extreme pain. He had been an active, positive person to whom many had turned for inspiration and help, but since his illness he had become passive and withdrawn. Because he didn't want to become dependant on pain killers and thus cloud his thinking, he was referred to Rabbi Twerski to try pain relief through hypnosis. This was not completely successful, but with the hypnotic trances, Rabbi Twerski was able to take the man back to his past to relive pleasurable and meaningful moments.

Eventually the man was using self-hypnosis two or three times a day, relaxing, going into a trance, and reexperiencing some enjoyable event of the past. His family noticed he had become a changed person and had regained much of his former personality.

Rabbi Twerski points out that what keeps most of us going is anticipation of good things in the future. What, then, can help the person who is terminally ill? For this person, there is little to look forward to. Reliving the past somehow changes this and once again makes life meaningful. There is enormous potential for helping terminal patients with the use of return tripping.

Victor Frankl, a psychiatrist, wrote about his experiences in the concentration camps:

> This intensification of inner life helped the prisoner find a refuge from the emptiness, desolation, and spiritual poverty of his existence by letting him escape into the past. When given free rein, his imagination played with past events, often not important ones, but minor happenings and trifling things.
>
> His nostalgic memory glorified them, and they assumed a strange character. Their world and their existence seemed very distant, and the spirit reached out for them longingly. In my mind I took

bus rides, unlocked the front door of my apartment, answered my telephone, switched on the electric lights. Our thoughts often centered around such details.

It is also important to do positive return tripping in order to provide balance for a person who has had a traumatic past. Even in the worst situations, everyone has some positive memories, and it is good to relive and strengthen them.

Often there is a resistance to remembering the good, and a person may keep saying, "No, everything was bad."

When asked to describe something good, Shira started her description of her overseas trip with the words "I suppose this was good, but I couldn't appreciate anything because I was so unhappy."

I asked Shira to describe each place she went to and revisit it, this time to appreciate its beauty or its art without the pervading feeling of gloom with which she had seen it before. We found she could eventually find inspiration in things she had seen and could actually become excited about them.

Situations that were too tense to appreciate at the time, like close family weddings, can be revisited and appreciated. Beautiful memories can be salvaged. It is amazing what experiences we store in our minds, ready for retrieval.

Chapter 2

FANTASY:
OUR OTHER SIDE

You are at a dinner to raise funds for a Jewish educational institution. You have been listening to several speakers, eaten far more than you usually would on a weekday evening, caught up on all the latest news, and are feeling somewhat drowsy.

On the table is the card you received upon entering. In the bottom lefthand corner is the number 277. The top lefthand corner, presumably with the same number, has been torn off.

Just then someone stands up and makes the announcement that the guests should look at their cards and note their number. After the next round of music he is going to announce the lucky winner of five thousand dollars.

You check your number again and listen to the music. It is a meditative tune, and you let the melody envelop your mind.

As the music fades, the master of ceremonies approaches the microphone and clears his throat. He is going to announce the winner! He pushes his hand into the depths of a large box and studies the corner of the card he has taken out.

He makes the announcement slowly and deliberately.

"The winner of the five thousand dollars is...ticket number...277."

You draw in your breath sharply. You look at your ticket, aware that your face has become a fiery red. You put up your hand, quite sure that at least ten other people in the hall must have the same number. The man repeats the number. Once more you look down at the card. Yes, it says most definitely 277.

You stand up and move slowly to the front of the hall, already, in your mind, spending the money on all kinds of things. You check the number over and over, and with a sudden rush of paranoia you look over your shoulder to make sure no one is planning to steal your card and run off with it.

You are approaching the front. People are cheering. You will soon be there to receive your prize. It is almost within your grasp.

But then you come back to yourself, and you realize that you are still seated at your table. The music is still playing, and they have yet to announce the winner. You realize that you did not win the five thousand dollars. You have been daydreaming, indulging in a flight of fancy.

We all go on them. Most of us feel that we have at least a few thoughts and emotions other people couldn't possibly have, fantasies we would never admit to, even to those closest to us, little thoughts that come into our minds just at the wrong moment.

Our minds have the habit of thinking the oddest things at the oddest moments, things we would not dream of thinking about. Let me give you an example:

One of your best friends calls to say he has just been given a senior position in his firm. He is ecstatic. His financial problems have been solved. He calls to tell you because you are his friend, and he wants to share the news with you. He expects you to be happy for him. And you are happy, you really are. He is your best friend, and you want the best for him.

But a thought creeps in from nowhere and whispers, *I hope it doesn't work out. He'll be disappointed, but he'll get over it.*

And then, shocked and horrified, you think, *How could I possibly have thought that? Of course I want him to be successful!*

And then another thought comes. *But it's a pity. Now he won't be struggling anymore. And we were struggling together.*

You berate yourself for your disloyalty to your friend. And you begin to wonder: *Was he really such a good friend? Do I really like him?*

Yes, he was and still is a friend, and you did and still do have love and affection for him. But very few things are totally pure in this world, and mixed with that love and affection are all kinds of jealousies and insecurities, which might be only a very small percentage of the relationship. They come out in these odd thoughts. Nevertheless, it does not detract from the very deep and genuine love you have for him.

We find examples in families. I might have a sister whom I love very much and for whom I would do anything.

One day she comes home crying bitterly, saying she has failed an exam. I am genuinely upset for her and really feel for her, and I want somehow to mend things for her. However, something else inside me says, *Too bad she failed, but it serves her right. She was doing far too well and making me feel like an absolute idiot. I'm sort of glad she failed actually...* I block out these thoughts, absolutely horrified at myself.

The love I feel for my sister is genuine and lasting. The fact that I have other fleeting thoughts in no way detracts from it. Many of us are surprised and shocked at ourselves for thinking such thoughts. Some of us feel self-recrimination. We find it difficult to accept these aspects of ourselves. We run from these thoughts, not wanting to look at them, until our guilt ruins our relationships and our self-esteem plummets. We have slid down a snake, and here we are, crouching at the bottom of the board.

It is important to realize that these thoughts come to everyone, no matter who they are. This is part of human nature and is a normal reaction. Surely a person who desires to refine his character and work on his *middos* can seize upon these odd, fleeting thoughts as an indication of areas that can be further strengthened through a daily *cheshbon hanefesh*, a spiritual accounting.

There are many accounts of tzaddikim who went out of their way to compensate for a moment of envy or anger. There is a well-known story about the Chafetz Chaim. When traveling, a fellow passenger, not knowing who the Chafetz Chaim was, went out of his way to annoy him. When he found out who he had annoyed, he was horrified and begged the Chafetz Chaim for forgiveness. The Chafetz Chaim went out of his way to give him a letter of recommendation to be a *shochet* to be sure he had eradicated any trace of anger.

A true effort toward character improvement must be based on a healthy self-esteem and acceptance of our frailties as human beings. Excessive self-doubt and obsessive self-criticism will produce not a spiritual master but rather a very disturbed and unbalanced individual.

One of our most common fantasies or daydreams (I have found that people are far more ready to admit to their dreams than their daydreams) is the drowning-rescue fantasy. In this fantasy we are the hero, and everything is done in front of people we desperately want to impress. It might run something like this:

You are leisurely strolling by a busy waterfront, and suddenly, coming in your direction, you see the managing director, the big boss, who hardly knows you exist. At that moment you see someone falling into the water. The person is drowning, and somehow no one else has noticed. You hesitate. Then you see the big boss looking at the person. Other people begin to shout. But no one moves. You dive into the water, swim to the floundering person, grab him, and swim back, using lifesaving techniques you learned in school. You drag him out of the water as a crowd gathers around watching. At the front of the crowd is the big boss. Next to him is someone else from the firm, one of the lesser bosses, who exclaims, "That man works for our firm in the accounts department!" The big boss looks at you approvingly. Then you faint from the exertion.

This daydream has endless variations. You could win a talent contest or be instrumental in averting a great disaster. You could be proclaimed the most outstanding artist or poet.

When people come to me for therapy, I concentrate a great deal on their fantasies and whatever occupies their thoughts during the day.

Very few of us never have these daydreams.

Very few of us would admit to them.

These thoughts come to everyone, no matter who he is. Many of us view these imaginings as our truest feelings and condemn ourselves for them. Because of this, self-accusations can accompany our most charitable actions.

Let's say you're walking with a friend, and someone approaches you for *tzedakah*. You reach into your pocket and give the man more than you would ordinarily. He smiles at you gratefully and you feel good. But then you start to analyze.

Why did I give more money than usual? Perhaps I wanted to impress my friend so he'd think I'm a big tzaddik. Or maybe I did it to ease my conscience. I had money, and the poor man did not. I felt guilty and to ease my guilt I gave him more than usual. What a poor motivation!

You may carry on with this train of thought and end up negating your whole mitzvah. Instead of feeling good about what you did, you feel worthless and ashamed.

It is important to understand that in most of our actions there is always a mixture of motivations. It is seldom that any of us have one hundred percent pure intentions in what we do, but the fact that there was a trace of wanting to impress our friend or ease our guilty conscience does not negate the fact that we gave because it is a mitzvah, and because of that our actions are commendable. Of course, as a person grows in Torah and mitzvos he should always strive to improve his *kavanah*, to search his heart for less worthy intentions and work toward doing every mitzvah for its own sake, *l'sheim Shamayim*. However, if you exaggerate the negative aspects of your motivations and allow them to eclipse your praiseworthy intentions, the next time you are asked to give *tzedakah* you will walk right past the needy person — and feel good about doing this — because you didn't give in to the temptation to impress your friend.

Daydreams and fantasies can also take us into dangerous places. You can inflame your fears until terror takes over. You can entertain thoughts of mistrust and suspicion of others until you begin to doubt those closest to you, and you may even destroy your relationships with them in this way — all because of fantasies of what they might be doing or might have done.

It may be that at first you know your suspicions are exaggerated. As time goes on, however, you begin to feel they might be true. Eventually, after giving your imagination free rein, you are certain your doubts are justified.

I once saw a professor berate his son for something he had not yet even done and probably never intended to do. The professor was trying to repair something, and, being more of an academic than a mechanic, he was not having much success.

His son offered to help, and the professor shouted at him. "I know what you'll do!" he yelled. "You'll play around and smash this delicate part over here, and then you'll wipe your hands of the whole thing, and I'll have to go to all kinds of expense to repair what you ruined."

The professor became so incensed at the thought that he did not speak to his son for two hours. Yet, as the son rightfully pointed out, he hadn't even touched anything. In fact, he had offered to help!

Another danger of thoughts losing touch with reality is when a person entertains the idea that he or she is a tzaddik, genius, or *gadol*. This person goes through life with a tremendous conflict. Every time he has an unworthy thought he tortures himself with feelings of guilt that are really rooted in pride. "How can *I*, a saint, be thinking *that*?" He cannot forgive himself or do any kind of real *teshuvah* because he won't let go of his fantasy. He agonizes over the imperfect thought that entered his "perfect" mind instead of working on himself and moving on.

Many people are perfectionists; they see things in black and white. A perfectionist can either be extremely positive or extremely negative. Things are either perfect or they're terrible. A perfectionist says to himself, perhaps unconsciously, "It's no good unless it's perfect."

Tzila is an example of this type:

"I always feel so inferior to other people. I always see them as better."

I looked at the tall, attractive, obviously intelligent girl in front of me.

"IN WHAT WAY ARE YOU INFERIOR? YOU ARE ATTRACTIVE AND CLEVER. YOU HAVE A GOOD JOB. ARE THESE PEOPLE BETTER THAN YOU IN ANY OF THESE THINGS?"

"No, not really. I just feel inferior."

"DO YOU FEEL INFERIOR TO OTHER PEOPLE, OR DO YOU FEEL YOU ARE INFERIOR TO AN ABSTRACT STANDARD OF A HUNDRED PERCENT?"

"Yes, yes! That's it! I feel I am not a hundred percent, and that is why I'm inferior."

"ARE OTHER PEOPLE A HUNDRED PERCENT?"

"No, not at all. They might even be forty percent or thirty percent but if I am not a hundred percent, I feel inferior to them all."

I have heard this many times: "If it's not perfect, it's no good at all."

Most of us have within ourselves something of the perfectionist in some area. The perfectionist can have great problems with unacceptable thoughts because he feels that these are part of him and make him less perfect. They torture themselves because of their thoughts until even the most innocent and good things in life are brought into question.

I treated an extremely talented, brilliant young man who had made a serious suicide attempt. Daniel explained that this happened because he was having unacceptable thoughts. While discussing this with him, it became clear that his thoughts had initially been only an occasional and fleeting occurrence. However, because of their unacceptability, he had become obsessive about them, and they had increased in frequency and intensity, taunting him all day.

Being a perfectionist, Daniel thought these thoughts were him and he suffered for months, unable to speak to anyone about it, planning his own destruction.

When I explained to him that all of us have strange thoughts and that this does not mean we will ever follow through with them, or have to identify with them, he began to get better. He began to look forward to life again, freed from his obsession with his improper fantasies.

There is another important factor with regard to day-dreams and fantasies. One of the most psychologically brilliant but simple sayings is "You can't stop birds from flying over your head, but you can stop them from making a nest in your hair."

There is a vast difference between thoughts that pop into our minds and thoughts we consciously fantasize about. We can learn to control what we think and how we really want to be. The oddest, most bizarre thoughts can come into your mind, but must you entertain these thoughts? Must you invite them in and have them to tea?

People may feel they have to follow up on whatever impulse comes to them, that they would somehow be harming themselves if they don't express and act on what they feel. They become caught up in all kinds of things and call it "freedom," but in reality they are allowing their emotions to lead them, and they become confused and disillusioned.

Real freedom is the freedom to say no, the freedom not to be swayed by every passing impulse. A person does not need to respond to every crazy idea or feeling that takes hold of him, nor does he have to be horrified at himself for thinking such things. You can look at a thought, examine it, and throw it out as unsuitable.

Many people believe that what they feel should be the reality. They want to be "true to their feelings" and follow through with them. We have to be aware that our feelings are far more under our control than we imagine, and that neither a thought nor a feeling can lead us into something we don't somehow want to become involved in.

Man is not fully conditioned and determined but

rather determines himself whether he gives in to conditions or stands up to them... Man does not simply exist but always decides what his existence will be, what he will become in the next moment... By the same token, every human being has the freedom to change at any instant.

(Eric Berne, Games People Play
[New York: Penguin Books, 1964], p. 32)

All of us know that we can control our fantasies, as if our minds were television sets that we could switch from a negative channel to a positive one. Most of the time we just don't choose to make the effort of turning that dial in the right direction.

Controlling our fantasies greatly increases our control on our lives. If we choose wisely where we go in our thoughts and fantasies, these are the places we will go to in reality.

Aaron T. Beck developed cognitive therapy, one of the most effective and popular therapies used today. It concentrates on how you think and how your thoughts affect you. It trains you to change the way you look at things and interpret them so as to feel better and act more productively.

Dr. Beck's theory is simple:

When you are depressed or anxious you are *thinking* in an illogical, negative manner, and you inadvertently act in a self-defeating way. With a little effort you can train yourself to straighten your twisted thought patterns. As your painful symptoms are eliminated you will become productive and happy again, and you will respect yourself.

These aims can usually be accomplished in a relatively brief period of time.

The Ten Cognitive Distortions

David Burns, a follower of Beck, enumerates ten cognitive distortions, twisted ways of thinking, which confuse us and make us vulnerable.

1. *All-or-nothing, black-and-white thinking.* We decide that we cannot tolerate anything less than perfection. We allow no gray areas. If a person is angry with us, he hates us. If we suffer a setback, a project becomes a complete failure. This distortion leads to the next one on the list.

2. *Overgeneralizing.* We see a single negative event as a never-ending pattern of defeat. If one apple is bad, the whole box is rotten. If the morning begins badly, the whole day is ruined.

3. *Dwelling on the negative.* We dwell on the negatives and ignore the positives. Sometimes we don't even *hear* the positives. If we hear constructive criticism which is ninety percent positive and ten percent is suggestions on how to improve, we see only the ten percent. We focus on the criticism rather than on the "constructive" part.

4. *Disqualifying the positive.* We insist that our positive qualities or accomplishments don't count. We have succeeded many times, but the only thing that stands out in our minds is the single time we failed.

5. *Jumping to conclusions.* We think we can read people's minds and inevitably conclude that they are thinking

badly of us. We also become convinced that things will turn out badly, even when there is absolutely no reason to think so.

6. *Magnifying or minimizing.* We blow up certain things and shrink others. Of course it's usually the negatives that get blown up and the positives that shrink, either in ourselves or in others.

7. *Emotional reasoning.* We judge from our feelings. "I feel like an idiot; therefore I must be one." "I feel terrible this morning, so I must look terrible and everyone can see it." "If I feel it, it must be true."

8. *Making "should" statements.* We criticize ourselves and others with words like *should* and *shouldn't.* This creates unnecessary guilt and resentment.

9. *Labeling and mislabeling.* We identify ourselves and others with specific shortcomings. Instead of saying, "I made a mistake" or "You forgot to lock the door," we say, "I never do anything right" or "You are such an idiot."

10. *Personalizing and blaming.* We either blame ourselves for something we weren't really responsible for, or we blame other people when our own attitude and behavior might have contributed to the problem.

In a later book, Burns teaches us how to untwist these ways of thinking:

1. *Identify the distortion.* Write down your negative thoughts, look at the list of ten cognitive distortions, and see if your thoughts fit into one or more of the categories.

2. *Examine the evidence.* If you feel you've never done

anything right, make a list — and be honest with yourself — of things you really have done successfully.

3. *Watch out for a double standard.* Instead of being harsh
with yourself, you should talk to yourself and about
yourself in the same compassionate way as you would
to a friend.

4. *Use the experimental technique.* Test the validity of your
negative thought. Let's say you have a fear of being hurt
in an elevator. Go into an elevator and see what happens. Hold your breath, jump up and down, and you'll
see that no harm will come to you.

5. *Think in shades of gray.* Evaluate things on a scale of 0
to 100. Don't view problems, achievements, and relationships in extreme terms.

6. *Employ the survey method.* Ask people questions to see
if your thoughts and attitudes are realistic. "Is everyone
nervous before public speaking, or is it only me?"

7. *Define your terms.* When you label yourself a loser you
can ask yourself, "What is the definition of a loser?" You
may see that there is no such thing.

8. *Use the semantic method.* Substitute milder and more
realistic terms for your emotionally colored language.

9. *Practice reattribution.* Instead of automatically assum-
ing you're at fault and blaming yourself for a certain
problem, see what else contributed to creating that
problem and then direct your energy into solving it.
There is no point in blaming yourself and feeling guilty.

10. *Do a cost-benefit analysis.* List the advantages and dis-
advantages of a feeling (such as getting angry when

your plane is late) or a behavior pattern (such as over-eating when you are feeling depressed) or a negative thought (such as "No matter how hard I try I always make a mess of things").

A thought can enter your mind and remain, so to speak, in the entrance, or you can bring the thought in, sit it down, and entertain it. Put up a sign that says DO NOT ENTER, and only welcome to your mind those thoughts that are productive.

Our thoughts determine our moods. Certain cognitive distortions will cause us to become angry and lose our motivation. By using Burns's advice on how to untwist our thinking we can be the masters of our thoughts instead of our thoughts being masters over us.

Chapter 3

SIFTING THE PAST
FOR ANGER

What is this snake that wends its way to the bottom of the board? It is the snake of suppressed anger and resentment.

Many of us don't let other people know when they have hurt or offended us. Instead of expressing it in a healthy way and discussing it, we bottle up our resentment and anger and withdraw, refusing to tell anyone what is wrong. We feel that people should be able to read our thoughts, and we create an atmosphere of seething bitterness. When we come into a room, everyone feels the tension.

We may act like a sulking child, but instead of pouting and sitting sullenly in the corner, we have adult variations of the same behavior. Here is one story to illustrate this common problem:

Sarah and Leah are at the airport, when suddenly Leah

freezes. A young woman with three children, looking sur-
prisingly like Leah, has entered the departure lounge.

Sarah follows the direction of her friend's gaze.
"Who's that?" she asks.

"Oh, a cousin of mine," says Leah in a rather cold
voice. "The daughter of my father's brother."

"No," she says sharply as Sarah starts to call, "don't
call her. We don't speak to each other. We have nothing
to do with that side of the family."

Sarah sits down, looking confused. "Her children
look the same age as your children. They could be such
good friends."

"Actually, I don't know how old they are," says Leah,
annoyed. "I don't think I even know their names."

"But what does your father say about this?" Sarah
asks curiously.

"It's my father and his brother who haven't spoken
in years — decades — so the family has no contact."

"What happened?" asks Sarah. "It must be something really dreadful."

"I'm not sure exactly," says Leah.

"Didn't you ask him?"

"Of course I did," says Leah, "but he doesn't seem to
be sure of it himself. Maybe he's forgotten. We just know
we must have nothing to do with that side of the family."

"She looks like you," says Sarah. "Why don't you
just go over and talk to her?"

We are familiar with stories of brothers kept apart because
of the Holocaust or the KGB, of families separated for many
years and don't even know the names and ages of one another's
children. But this time the brothers themselves have created

the distance through resentment and bitterness. They have even forgotten what the initial breach was about.

In South Africa, we call this a *fariebel*. Everyone knows what a *fariebel* is. This person won't speak to that person and that person will have nothing to do with this person, and these *fariebel*s can go on for years, splitting families and former friends. Sadly, when someone is making a *simchah*, she has to find out who is having a *fariebel* with whom so as not to seat them near each other.

Expressing Anger

Let's take a closer look at anger. When we become angry, we may express it in several ways. A person, especially a child, may express it directly, by hitting or punching, or indirectly, by breaking things or slamming doors. He might become verbally abusive, either directly or indirectly. Alternatively, one might channel one's aggression into positive actions or lose his temper quickly but get over it easily.

I wish to focus on the person who becomes angry at another but refuses to explain what has angered him. He withdraws, filled with hurt, resentment, and hatred. In his mind, the offense builds into something greater and more monstrous as he tries to justify his feelings. The offending friend or relative may ask what is wrong, but he refuses to tell him, feeling that just as it pervades his mind, so should it be clearly visible to the friend. How could he not know? After a while, the friend, too, withdraws. The rift becomes wider and wider, and bitterness holds a corrosive grip on the angry person.

A woman once came to me for therapy. On many occasions her father accompanied her, which was very strange, as you will see.

Sometime during one of the sessions she mentioned that her father appeared to be quite friendly and caring, but for the past fifteen years he had been in her home for only a few minutes at a time and consistently refused all invitations to eat with her family. This upset her very much.

I asked why this was so. She replied that she had no idea. I asked her permission to speak to her father and called him in alone. He became very emotional, telling me that fifteen years ago his daughter had said something that had hurt his feelings and he had decided not to eat in her house until he received an apology. I asked him if his daughter was aware of this, and he shook his head, repeating again that until she apologized he would not eat in her home. I then requested his permission to speak with her.

When she heard what her father had said, the woman was astounded. She claimed she had known nothing about this and would, of course, apologize.

I brought the father in, the daughter apologized, and he burst into tears, saying he had waited for this for fifteen years.

This woman's father had lived with his bitterness and hurt all those years and deprived himself and his family of so much time together — and he did not even tell his daughter why. All that time he was waiting for her apology, and she didn't even know she had anything to apologize for.

I told this story to one of my student groups and asked if anyone in the class was harboring resentment for someone and not speaking about it. One of the girls volunteered that she had been a good friend of another girl in the class, but they had not communicated for over a year. She mentioned the name of the girl, who turned to her in astonishment.

"I know you have become less friendly, and you don't want to talk to me, but I don't know why."

"You kicked me," said the student.

The second student frowned, trying to search her memory. "I didn't," she said at last. "When did I kick you?"

The student mentioned the occasion, and the other girl looked at her in horror. "I didn't kick you. I tripped over you. And I said I was sorry at the time, didn't I?"

Needless to say, they sorted it out and have once again become friends, but the estrangement could so easily have gone on.

If we sift through our past, we will probably find several people we have grown distant from because they hurt us. Some of us are more prone to this pattern than others, but it affects most people to some degree.

Perhaps we don't go to the extreme of cutting off our close relatives or friends, but we could still be losing out on friendships which could be more rewarding and fulfilling. We may feel resentful or bitter after having assumed a person meant "this" when in fact he meant "that." But the real damage is done to ourselves. Bitterness affects us on a spiritual, as well as on an emotional and even on a physical, level. Deep-seated resentment can weaken our immunity and make us prone to all kinds of illnesses.

Recent research carried out by the Cardiac Rehabilitation Unit in Johannesburg has found that patient noncompliance can often be attributed to pent-up bitterness and aggression. People who are seriously ill may not follow their doctor's instructions, refusing to take their medication properly or failing to adhere to dietary regimes. It seems negative baggage can interfere with a person's natural instinct to take care of his health. Resentment can also cause a person to be anxious, depressed, and pessimistic and never able to find real pleasure in anything he does.

I see many people who have a critical and unhappy attitude. They may appear pleasant and sociable on the surface, but they have a tendency to dampen the enthusiasm of others and to throw a cloud of guilt and gloom on any carefree situation or conversation. These are people who have built up a great deal of anger over the years and have never expressed it appropriately. They may have inappropriate outbursts or attacks directed against themselves.

These destructive emotions affect the person they are directed at very minimally compared with the devastating effects they have on the person harboring them. It is the one who hates, rather than the one who is hated, who truly suffers.

Many people, knowing that the Torah compares anger to idol worship and condemns it in the extreme, think they must bottle up their anger until it becomes a seething mass of hatred and bitterness. They accept insults and smile outwardly, but their internal storehouse boils.

I saw this anonymous quotation on someone's notice board: "Anger and bitterness do more harm to the vessel in which it is stored than the vessel over which it is poured."

Letting Go of Anger

Let us take a second look at the murky red snake of suppressed anger and resentment.

A person can discharge his anger in many different ways,

not necessarily with an aggressive outburst. Even laughter can dissolve anger, just as a good bout of crying can.

As Torah Jews enjoined to stay far away from anger, it is important to remember: Anger does not always have to be *let out*. It can also be *let go*.

When you feel you're being strangled by the python of hate, you have to look through your past to find out what made you angry and view those experiences again with new eyes. Sift through your memories with a sieve that catches only resentment and bitterness and analyze the situations that provoked it. As you do this you will find a ladder leading to positive places you never imagined existed. At times a person who does this realizes his anger was not necessary. His more mature mind can see what the child did not, and in this way he can let go.

A person may find he can finally forgive the offending party, or he may find that although he still has to work on forgiving, he can now let go of his anger. However, it is up to each person to be willing to let go — to let go of his anger and to embark on an extensive cleanup of the past. Such a commitment in itself is often half the journey.

Batsheva was forty-eight, a fairly attractive woman, who had always taken good care of herself. The lines around her mouth, however, were a telltale sign of the bitterness and resentment she held inside. She was oversensitive and easily offended, depressed, agitated, and moody.

It took a long time before she was willing to start looking at the past to pinpoint and let go of her anger. For several reasons, she felt the need to hold on to it and seemed to imagine that the letting go of all her anger and resentment would leave a terrible emptiness.

Batsheva was the eldest of three children, and when she came to me for therapy, we began with the jealousy and resentment she felt toward her younger siblings and the fact that she had been blamed for everything they did. If she fought with them or they fought with her, she was always put in the wrong by her parents because she was the eldest. If they destroyed her books or possessions, they were excused.

As we discussed these issues, she began to realize that this happens to most firstborn children, but that there were also many advantages to being the oldest, which she was able, for the first time, to recognize and appreciate. She was always first in line for clothes, which for her sisters became hand-me-downs. And she had privileges the others never had.

She also bitterly resented the fact that her mother had given away her dog. We dealt with this situation in actuality, for she was able to speak with her mother, who was still alive. Her mother told her that the dog had bitten a child down the road, but she had not wanted to tell her this at the time. (Often solutions can be found by speaking to the people concerned and gaining new information. Raising her own children made Batsheva view many of her early life situations with a great deal more tolerance and understanding, and she was better able to understand her own mother's actions.)

As we reviewed Batsheva's youth, we encountered teachers who had had favorites. Batsheva was able to understand and forgive them. She let go of the anger toward a friend who had chosen a different girl to be her best friend. She sifted through as much of her childhood as she could, discovering, forgiving, understanding, or just letting go. After several of these sessions, Beverly had begun to develop a certain quality of softness and sensitivity. As she progressed through her adolescence, her marriage, and its subsequent breakup, she felt lighter, more free. Other people began to respond to her and enjoy her company.

Batsheva was on the path to true personal freedom.

I found a similar reaction with Malka. After several sessions, Malka suddenly became tearful.

"My parents never showed me they really cared or that I was in any way special to them. I can't say I was ill treated. I was just not important. They looked after me like they looked after the plants.

"Everything looked good to the outsider, but it wasn't any bed of roses."

I stopped Malka and examined that last statement.

"PERHAPS IT REALLY WAS A BED OF ROSES. WHAT DO YOU THINK IT WOULD BE LIKE TO LIE DOWN IN A BED OF ROSES?"

"What?" Malka laughed. "You mean the thorns? It would be painful, even though it would look so lovely."

"THEN PERHAPS IT WAS A BED OF ROSES AFTER ALL."

Malka came to understand that it was not easy for any of the family to live in this rose bed. Each member was facing his own challenges and troubles. Malka began to approach the members of her family, to get to know them as people and somehow alleviate the pain and root out the anger.

People have often responded with great enthusiasm and intense relief to this form of sifting for anger. Malka's problem of anger over the apparent indifference of key people in her childhood environment is not an unusual one at all.

Malka knew what was bothering her and she knew she was angry. However, in many instances the anger is masked by other complicated feelings.

When Carol came to see me she seemed ill at ease. She would shift in her chair and remain silent for a time. But the silence made her feel more uneasy, and she would attempt to break it.

"I can't remember anything. My mind is just a big blank."

"TELL ME ABOUT A FAVORITE TOY YOU HAD. TRY TO DESCRIBE IT TO ME."

She was silent for a minute and then suddenly smiled.

"It was a stuffed dog. It was supposed to be white, but I hardly let anyone take it away from me to wash it, so it turned a grayish brown. I always took it to bed with me at night. Sometimes I couldn't find it, and I would wander around, becoming more and more anxious, until my brother and sister helped me look for it and, as I became more upset, my mother and finally my father.

"One night we all became quite desperate. I was exhausted, but I couldn't go to sleep without my dog. I can't remember what happened in the end. I must have found it. And I think this happened more than once. It really must have been quite funny to see." She started to laugh and then stopped suddenly.

"Actually I always thought my parents were far too

busy to really become involved in what I was doing, but this shows that on some occasions, at least, they had to take notice."

I asked her why she felt they were too busy to become involved with her, but again she fell silent.

I asked her if she remembered the way the family had spent their time — what she, her mother, her father, her brother, and her sister usually did when she was a child.

"My father was a real-estate agent, and he was always busy when I was home. I suppose people can buy houses only at funny hours. Sunday was show house day, and he would be gone all day till quite late in the evening.

"My mother was home at the right times. She only worked in the mornings, but she was always sewing or reading or typing.

"My younger brother and sister were always around, playing or fighting. I never really joined them, because their games were babyish and boring. But they had each other to play with.

"We would be woken up at around 6:30 A.M. by my mother, get dressed for school, and have breakfast. My mother always fed us well and gave us a lot of school lunch, but she didn't speak to us much, especially in the morning.

"If I tried to discuss anything, she would say, 'Don't talk now. You'll be late for school.' I often wondered when I could discuss anything with her, because at night I had to go to bed and during the day she was always busy."

It took quite a few sessions before Carol even recognized

that she was resentful and bitter. Only after seeing this could she let go of the anger, by trying to understand her family and accept them. It was as if she had cut off and negated a part of her life and was now reclaiming it. As a result, her personality became richer, and she grew more confident.

People do not always acknowledge their anger, and in many instances they cut off the person they are angry with without even acknowledging that they are angry. It is as though the offending person no longer exists and the relationship is often gone forever.

> Boo hoo hoo, I'm a lonely croc
> lying all day on a sunny rock...
> I've eaten all the friends I know
>
> *(A children's song)*

Most of us have had good friends, even close relatives, who we no longer see. We feel they have somehow hurt us or failed us, and we have cut them off — forever. Harsh words have been exchanged and may now be hardly remembered, but the person remains "on ice," wrapped up in a great deal of hurt.

Return trip therapy allows a person to go on a search-and-find mission for lost family and friends. Those last words are explored, analyzed, and perhaps understood in a completely different light. The person may begin to warm up to the estranged friend, and often relationships are reinstated and families united, with a deeper appreciation and understanding of one another.

In the Alcoholics Anonymous twelve steps book it says: "We had to see that when we harbored grudges and planned revenge we were really beating ourselves with the club of anger we had intended to use on others."

Miriam was an extremely attractive, intelligent girl who gave the impression of being independent and self-sufficient. She appeared to have many friends and was seldom alone.

During the first interview with me, however, it became obvious that she nursed a very deep loneliness. She had somehow managed to cut off all close ties and kept contact to a cold minimum. She had a different story about each of her family members. Each one had hurt her at one time or another, so each one had been "killed off" by her emotionally.

She searched for the ropes of anger, carefully unknotting and extracting them, and then she began the practical work of bringing the relationships back to life.

Miriam met with her parents, and in a sense it was for the first time. She began to contact old friends. Where there did seem to be a very valid reason for her anger, she would discuss it with the friends, usually to find that what she had understood had not been meant at all. Regarding people who could not be contacted, she found the answers within herself by returning to the past and trying to understand.

One thing she decided to do in the future was to try to sort out misunderstandings and quarrels immediately, or at least as soon as her initial anger had subsided. She learned to say, "You hurt me with what you said. Do you realize that?" or, "I feel upset or offended when you say things like that."

Miriam found that she was better able to get close to people. She also learned that a truly good relationship is not destroyed by misunderstandings and disagree-

ments, and that one can argue with a person and remain close, with the interpersonal bond staying strong. She came to realize that she could be criticized out of love and that this in no way altered a relationship. She realized that what she kept saying to people was "I'm afraid that one day you'll get angry at me, and then you won't want anything to do with me."

It took a long time to convince herself that even if people got mad at her sometimes they would continue to like her, and certainly not lose respect for her. She found she could irritate others at times without in any way affecting a relationship.

For some reason, the fact that people can fight and still remain close is a difficult lesson for many to understand. When I was seeing children for therapy, I found that their best friend was invariably the child they fought with most.

I am not, of course, advocating constant fighting but rather straight talking. There's a certain creative fighting which ends in a stronger bond and often in positive action. I am not talking about destructive fighting which can destroy relationships and exhaust people, both emotionally and physically. Aggression is not always negative. If expressed in a constructive, honest, and creative way, it has a great deal of positive force to it.

> It's natural to believe that external events upset you. But other people cannot make you angry... The bitter truth is that you're the one who's creating every last ounce of the outrage you experience.
>
> (David Burns, Feeling Good: The New Mood Therapy
> [New York: Signet Books, 1981], p. 139)

Which cognitive distortions can lead to anger? Labeling, overgeneralizing, and "monsterizing." We write people off. We use false targets for anger. We practice mind-reading and invent motives for the other person and magnify all of these. We blow things out of proportion.

Three main sources of anger are:

1. When you are blocked from achieving a valued goal, for example, missing a bus. You may think, *It's not fair. It shouldn't have happened.*

2. When someone has broken one of your personal rules; for example, you may have decided you should be treated politely at all times. This is unrealistic and won't always happen.

3. When your self-esteem is threatened; for example, someone may criticize your work. Your defensive burst of temper protects you from considering that perhaps the criticism was justified.

Each of these brands of anger is rooted in misconception. Once we recognize which cognitive distortions have led us to become angry, we can tackle the various breaches in our personal life. Those with courage can break the ice with a phone call or letter, or even approach the estranged person directly. Others may choose to enlist a third party to act as mediator. If you have many relationships which have been "put on ice," you could begin by making contact with just one person and then, when you see the profound difference it makes in your life, follow up with more.

The rewards are immeasurable on every level. You become more at peace with yourself and the world. You may also find friendships made richer by what you have gone through together.

It is important to understand that a healthy reconciliation does not mean you are negating your own feelings and letting others walk all over you. You can be assertive without being aggressive and present your opinion in an acceptable way without resorting to nastiness or belittling the other person. When you are hurt or offended, you may say so in a way which clears the air rather than clouds it with confusion and bitterness. A person can be forceful and strong in the most quiet, gentle way.

Being Assertive

If we don't let people know when we are hurt or upset, they won't realize how we feel and there is little hope of sorting things out. The anger within us becomes stale and ugly, eroding our well-being. We have to learn to tell people when they hurt our feelings and not be afraid. There are many excellent books on assertive techniques. Using these methods can change a person's life completely and free him to be himself in a world he no longer sees as hostile. I will discuss some of these methods briefly.

You don't have to be rude or aggressive to get your needs met, but you do have to learn how to be assertive. You will find that you will not be rejected for being yourself.

The key is knowing what you want and that you have the right to ask for what you want. When you are assertive, you are conscious of your basic rights as a human being. You give yourself and your particular needs the same respect and dignity you would give to anyone else's.

By striking a balance between aggressiveness and submissiveness, you are able to get your needs met in a way that preserves the dignity of others.

Here are four signs of a truly assertive person:

1. He feels free to reveal himself. "This is who I am. This is how I think, what I feel, what I want."

2. He can communicate with people of all ages and walks of life in an open, direct, honest, and appropriate manner.

3. He has an active approach to life and goes after what he wants. He makes things happen rather than waiting for them to happen.

4. He acts in a way that he himself can respect.

What is the difference between aggression, passivity, and assertiveness?

Aggression: "What I say is right, and your opinion doesn't count." Here we are standing up for personal rights and feelings in an inappropriate way. We violate the rights of others. We attack and blame.

Passivity: "I don't count. You can take advantage of me." We find it difficult to disagree or to say no. We are afraid to upset others or worry about what they might think. Here we are violating our own rights and not expressing thoughts and feelings honestly, or we are doing so in such an apologetic way that our words are disregarded. We may act helpless and try to get others to act for us. We may express our feelings in a dishonest way by speaking *lashon hara* or making others feel guilty.

Assertiveness: This is the direct, honest, and appropriate expression of opinions, beliefs, needs, or feelings. We stand up for our rights in a way that does not impinge upon the rights of others.

Some people try never to hurt anyone by concealing their feelings, but inevitably they hurt more people more deeply. They destroy relationships by not letting people know what they really feel. People take advantage of them without realizing it, and they become filled with seething, unexpressed resentment.

One of the most difficult things in the world for some of us is to say no, because we're afraid people won't like us. But this is an important skill for anyone who wants to become assertive. Saying no means that you can *set limits* on other people's demands for your time and energy when such demands conflict with your own needs and desires. It also means that you can do this without feeling guilty. Usually "no, thank you" or "I'm not interested" is enough, but if they persist you can look the person in the eye and firmly repeat, "I'm sorry, but I have to say no," or, "I wish I could participate, but it's going to be impossible."

Here are a few techniques that can help you:

1. *The broken-record technique.* You keep repeating what you have to say no matter what the response. Let's say you bought a tape recorder which doesn't work. You go back to the store and explain, "This machine is faulty. I want you to replace it." The salesmen argues and you just repeat, "Yes but this machine is faulty. It must be replaced." This can go on and on until he gives in. After all, if you remain calm and show that you're willing to stand there all day, the pressure will be on the salesman. Does he really want you there in his store all day long?

Evaluate your rights. Once you are sure of what you want to achieve and what you are entitled to, you can voice a firm, simple request without apology, and in a nonjudgmental, non-blaming manner. You should always request, not demand or plea. It is best to use "I" statements, such as "I ordered a different color" or "I would like a replacement, not a repair." If you must take issue with the service you have received, always object to specific behaviors, not to the personalities of those involved.

If the person keeps refusing to accede to your request, you could ask an assertive question such as "Is there a reason you're having such a hard time with my request?"

2. *Fogging*. When you are confronted with a negative statement, calmly repeat it.

"You really irritate me."

"I really irritate you."

3. *Defusing*. When someone gets angry with you, let him express it. Listen without becoming defensive and then tell him you'll talk to him later. This gives him a sense of being heard and helps him calm down. You gain time to think over the matter instead of answering in the heat of the moment. When both of you are calm, there is a better chance of coming to an understanding.

These techniques will help a person express himself without becoming angry and preserve the precious relationships in his life.

Chapter 4

COPING WITH STRESS AND TENSION

Anxiety has been described as a pervasive feeling of dread, apprehension, and impending disaster. Fear is a response to a clear and present danger. Anxiety is a response to an undefined or unknown threat which in many cases stems from conflicts within ourselves. In both, however, the body mobilizes itself to meet the threat, and muscles become tense, breathing is faster, and the heart beats more rapidly.

(Robert M. Goldenson, Dictionary of Psychology and Psychiatry [New York and London: Longman, 1984])

Anxiety has been called the "black sheep in the family of fear." Fear has a definite object which can be faced, analyzed, attacked, or endured. With anxiety, on the other hand, the object is unknown.

People often feel they are caught up in a whirlpool of stress, tension, and anxiety. I see this whirlpool as another snake, a python that twines around and around you until you feel you have no freedom to move or breathe. We have to find ways of freeing ourselves of this snake.

Some obvious sources of stress are loss, drastic changes of location and responsibilities, the threat of serious illness, or lasting disability and other emotionally charged events. However, stress is not something which occurs due to outside sources alone. Much of it has to do with what goes on within a person when he is faced with these challenges.

Stress need not be seen as something totally negative. In fact, all life requires a certain amount of stress or stimulation in order for us to function at our best. If we removed all tension from a person's body, he would drop to the floor and not be able to get up. The problem comes when a person wants to constantly function at top pitch, like an engine always going full speed ahead. People have the mistaken impression that by being in a constant state of preparedness and tension they will accomplish more and be more effective in everything they do. Many studies have shown this to be false. An increase in tension and anxiety stifles creativity. You'd be surprised to find how much more you could accomplish if the tension were reduced.

Because of tension, many in the Western world have forgotten how to enjoy life. Even in our leisure time we may subject ourselves to prolonged sensory bombardment rather than enjoy a period of quiet. Within this context of haste and perpetual stimulation, the average human being moves from task to task with almost no time to just *be*, to get in touch with himself, to relax.

People have often been accused of either living in the past or in the future. They forget about the here and now and concentrate on what is around the corner. They are never *here* because they are always *there*. They cannot truly concentrate on what they're doing, and life becomes empty and meaningless, filled with stress and tension. In this way, a person constantly chases time and never quite catches it.

The Symptoms of Stress

When a person is in danger, he has a fight or flight reaction, with increased blood pressure, sweating, and rapid breathing. Muscles tense. The reactions are automatic; you don't have to think about it. The body produces enough energy to either run away or do amazing things, such as jumping over a high wall, which could never be done in ordinary circumstances.

However, stress of all kinds, inner and outer, can make a person's body react in this way at inappropriate times. A person can, in a sense, be constantly poised for fight or flight. In this case the person will have all sorts of symptoms. He may feel sick, have butterflies in his stomach or a jelly-like sensation in his legs, aching muscles, headaches, a racing or thumping heart, or he may experience fidgeting or clumsiness. He might have indigestion or lose his appetite, feel tingling in his limbs, ringing in his ears, choking sensations, a lump in his throat, shortness of breath, and clammy hands. Blood pressure may rise or drop.

Anxious and tense people tend to have gloomy, pessimistic thoughts and poor views of themselves. This increases their anxiety and makes feared situations worse. They feel keyed up and have constant feelings of uneasiness.

There is such a thing as a fear of fear. People who are anxious can become even more frightened by the physical manifestations of their anxiety. In response to their anxiety and tension, they may overeat or rush through meals, drink or smoke too much, overwork, become argumentative, become restless, irritable, and generally difficult to handle at work and at home. They are not at peace within themselves.

When anxiety and stress levels rise to a very high pitch, it is common for a person to become afraid of everyday activities like going on buses, shopping, or even being alone at home. The tension can change his or her physical reality, thoughts and outlook on life, behavior, and lifestyle.

Constant tension and stress have proven detrimental to one's physical health. Most, if not all, major diseases are tension-related. Heart disease, cancer, strokes, ulcers, migraines, and skin diseases have all been linked to stress, as well as a general susceptibility to infections. In fact, considerable evidence is being collected demonstrating a relationship between stress and immune functions. Until recently people suffering from illnesses saw themselves as being the helpless victims of invading microbes and viruses. There is now a shift in perception. We can alter the odds in our favor if we'd realize that stress is a major factor in our health.

Panic Attacks

What would you think if the man sitting across from you on the bus turned pale and started shaking? What if he told you he was having trouble breathing and having pains in his chest? Wouldn't you think he is having a heart attack? But it could very well be that he is having a panic attack, which can be caused by a build-up of stress.

Perhaps the most crippling anxiety experience is the panic attack. A person experiences sudden and overwhelming terror, palpitations, rapid heartbeat, chest pain, trembling, faintness, dizziness, and the sensation that he is suffocating. The attacks appear irrational, their intensity out of proportion to whatever triggered them.

When the person experiences his first attack, he may be afraid that he's dying or losing his mind. He may be reassured by a medical checkup, but with the next attack, and the next, he begins to build up a fear of the panic itself. He may not want to leave home for fear of having an attack in public. Often he hyperventilates, breathing too fast, which leads to dizziness and increases the panic.

I always sympathized with people who have panic attacks, but never really understood until the day I had one myself.

Several of my family members had been extremely ill within a short space of time, and I had been overdoing it, running between my patients and the hospitals. I lay down one evening for a five-minute rest before I had to go out again, when an overwhelming feeling of panic settled over me. My body felt strange and I was shaking. I thought I would faint or even die.

I called the doctor, and he told me it sounded like a panic attack, and when I asked him rather sheepishly if he was sure, he replied, "Never mind. It will help you understand your patients better."

It certainly did.

What can one do about panic attacks? There are various forms of therapy.

The traditional form of behavior therapy has been found

to be very effective in some panic disorders, especially where the person has become agoraphobic and is afraid to drive the car, go shopping, or go in elevators. By a process that is known as deconditioning, the person is slowly taught to do these things again. Many people find relief in relaxation techniques, and group therapy often helps, especially when the person realizes that others have experienced similar symptoms. If the condition is very severe, a person may be given medication, such as small doses of an antidepressant.

Here are a few simple suggestions of what you can do in the event of a panic attack:

- First, it is important to remind yourself of certain facts. A panic attack can't kill you, and you will not die during a panic attack. You will not faint, go mad, or damage yourself physically. You should also tell yourself that this is a normal physical reaction, but you are feeling it in the wrong situation.

- Focus on what is *really* happening in your body at that moment, not what *might* happen. Many of the most frightening sensations we experience in a panic attack like the feeling of being out of control or that we are going to die are the result of hyperventilation.

- Don't fight these feelings. Rather, give them a chance to go away slowly. Later, when the attack has subsided, try to resume what you were doing before it started.

- Slowing down and controlling your breathing slows down your system and can prevent or relieve panic attacks and other feelings of intense anxiety and tension. Breathe out slowly and gently, so that the flow of air would not disturb a feather attached to the tip of your nose. A restful stillness will be generated through deep breathing.

Here is one exercise for deep breathing:

1. Find a comfortable position in a chair or bed in a quiet room.

2. Relax as much as possible.

3. Try to become aware of your breathing.

4. Place your hands on your stomach.

5. Breathe in for a slow count of three, expanding the stomach.

6. Hold your breath for a slow count of three.

7. Breathe out for a slow count of three, flattening the stomach.

8. Relax your shoulders, pushing them forward and down.

Repeat this rhythm two or three times at first, gradually increasing the number of times until you can breathe this way for several minutes. Practice this every day.

Another method used to cope with panic attacks is to choose a focus word or phrase, for example *peace* or *I'm calm*. Sit quietly, relax your body, and breathe slowly and deeply. Say the focus word or phrase each time you exhale. If you lose concentration, simply wait for the distracting thoughts to pass through your mind, then return to your focus word. Continue for five minutes at a time, gradually increasing to twenty minutes. Do this routine at least once a day. Such relaxation exercises, done regularly, can slow your breathing rate, decrease your oxygen consumption, calm your brain-wave rhythms, and lower your blood pressure.

If you realize you are breathing rapidly or hyperventilating, blow on your hand and count five seconds — one and two and three and four and five and — then take a normal breath and do it again.

Return trip therapy can be very effective in finding the precipitating cause of panic attacks. I used this method with Aharon, who was experiencing repeated anxiety attacks. I asked him to think back to his childhood and actually see himself.

Aharon stared into space for some minutes. "Yes," he said. "I can picture my room. I never thought I could see things so clearly. The bedspread, turquoise, which kept putting fluff on my school blazer, my carpet, a sort of mat, really, with a lion on it.

"I had a tall, thin cupboard where I kept all my games, Monopoly, Scrabble, checkers. One of the cupboard doors was loose, but you didn't notice it if you shut it a certain way. My father was always saying he would fix it, but he never did, and then it was too late..."

"DO YOU REMEMBER THE DAY YOUR FATHER DIED?"

"Pretty much. I think I was doing homework. Math. I hated it. All of a sudden I heard my mother screaming — she sounded like an animal. I was paralyzed with fear. I knew I should go see what was wrong, but I was frightened. I thought she was being attacked, and I was afraid if I went to rescue her I would get attacked myself, so I just sat there."

Aharon spoke in a whisper so I had to strain my ears to hear him.

"I have never, ever told this to anyone. I have never even admitted it to myself. Anyway, the screaming stopped, and at the same time a neighbor came into the house and called me. He said my father was very ill and was being taken to the hospital. I remember the sick feeling I had because I knew he was not telling me the truth.

"The ambulance came, and that night I went to sleep at a friend. I think my mother went to a friend, too.

"I remember the funeral. They hadn't wanted me to come, but I insisted. For many, many nights I would remember the coffin being lowered into the ground. I would hear the sound of the earth hitting the wood. I could not believe that someone so strong and so alive could suddenly be under the ground. I thought there must be some mistake.

"I became terribly afraid — afraid that something would happen to me. I began to feel dizzy and sick and pictured dying and being buried. Even at yeshivah I would sometimes stop hearing what the rebbe was saying and start reliving the burial.

"I still feel sick and giddy when I think about it. I've always thought of myself as a coward. And I never had anyone to speak to..."

I told Aharon that we could go back to talk to that child and to listen to him. Return trip therapy helped Aharon get rid of his fear, and his panic attacks disappeared.

Alleviating Stress

The Torah teaches us to guard our health and to avoid those things which are detrimental to it. With this in mind we have an obligation to recognize when we feel stress and tension and do what we can to alleviate it.

Methods used to cope with stress can be negative or positive. Negative ways include overspending, complaining, and overeating. Obviously such behavior ultimately leads to increased tension and stress.

Positive ways include talking things out with someone, especially a good friend. Crying can also reduce stress or thinking through problems logically and working them out in a positive way. Laughter is one of the best ways to reduce stress.

What can you do when you are under stress and your mind is filled with negative thoughts? Work on substituting those thoughts with positive, happy thoughts. You can control the thoughts in your mind. If a negative thought passes through your mind, send it swiftly on its way.

To gain control of your thoughts and clear your mind you can do the following exercise. All you need is twenty minutes of uninterrupted time.

Sit comfortably in a chair with your eyes closed. Put on your favorite music, with earphones, if possible. Concentrate on the music. Picture yourself sitting on a sandy mound on the beach, watching the waves breaking against the shore. The sun is warm and you are at peace...

After an interlude like this, you come back to earth refreshed, with a strange sense that the twenty minutes were more like two hours.

Taking time out to sit quietly is essential. You can shut your eyes and travel anywhere. You can rest on the banks of a clear stream. You can sit on a sandy beach and watch the waves lapping at the shore. You can walk along mountain paths.

In your mind, you can picture a shady tree. You can lie under it, looking up through its thick, leafy branches. You can see the sun peeping through, dancing in flickers of light through the leaves. The grass you are lying on is soft. You can even hear a bird singing and spot him far above in one of the thinner branches...

Some people find it helpful to play a piece of orchestral music and go with it wherever it leads them, again while shutting their eyes and sitting in a relaxed position.

Some people experience a free-floating type of anxiety where they just cannot relax, and this interferes with their sleep. Going on trips at bedtime can help with these sleep problems. It can be a self-created bedtime story.

You can decide, before you go to bed, exactly where you want to go. Use the same relaxation methods mentioned above, but do it just before you are about to fall asleep.

People have many reasons why they cannot sleep.

One woman made this strange claim: "I spent my early years sleeping in a cage."

When I looked startled, she explained, "It was really a portable air-raid shelter which fit into our bedroom. If a bomb would drop on the house, whoever was in the shelter would be protected."

These shelters were common during the Second World War in England. The shelter was made of steel and looked like a cage with a heavy steel roof and bars. This was protection from bombs so that if a building collapsed the shelter would remain intact and the people inside could be dug out.

"My brother and I both slept in the shelter, and my mother made her bed on top of it, saying that if the air-raid sirens went off, she would come inside with us.

"I remember night after night filled with guilt and fear, for we were safe and my mother was in danger. I often begged her to come inside because I couldn't bear the tension, but she said she didn't like closed places and would rather sleep on top.

"I think this is what made me so anxious and so afraid of letting go in order to sleep. I've had sleeping problems ever since and have been taking sleeping pills for years."

We did return trip therapy, but we also did a program to help her relax so she could fall asleep more naturally. She would also do this soon after her husband had gone to work and the children had gone to school so she could face her morning free of anxiety.

All of us experience anxiety and tension of one kind or another, and we have to set small havens for ourselves where we can go in our minds to pleasant, peaceful, inspiring places.

Relaxation exercises are also extremely important for reducing stress. There are various methods where a person is taught to recognize tension in different parts of the body and relax his muscles progressively and systematically. Later he can be taught to relax his mind or his racing thoughts.

An alternative is aromatherapy, particularly using the essential oil of lavender. There are also various herbal therapies, such as relaxing herbal teas, capsules, or tinctures.

Vigorous aerobic exercise can reduce the level of pulse-quickening hormones released during stress and at the same time stimulate a sense of well-being. Even a brisk walk around the block can help reduce anxiety. Stretching exercises can relax tense upper-body muscles that accompany stress and affect breathing.

You may wish to consider preventative measures. Cultivate outside interests and plan occasional diversions to break your routine. Set up a regular sleeping schedule and get plenty of rest without the use of sleeping pills. Exercise regularly and vigorously, as appropriate for your age. Avoid hurry and worry, which can upset your sleeping, eating, and other vital functions. Take time to relax and enjoy life.

Make a list of what troubles you. For each issue, ask yourself: What's the worst thing and the best thing that can happen? Have I done what I can to prepare for both? Is this problem really worth worrying about?

Laugh more and at all costs avoid self-pity. One of my patients made a small card for me that said, "Laughter is a tranquilizer with no side effects."

Learn to reestablish your equilibrium after a stressful event. Make an effort to reach out to others.

When you're facing a stressful situation, remember a bit of folk wisdom: Count to ten and take a deep breath before saying or doing anything. A deliberate pause can be an instant tranquilizer.

How do you wake up in the morning? Do you jump out of bed already worried about being late for work or school? It may be better to wake up fifteen minutes earlier to make time to organize things in a relaxed way than to spend those fifteen minutes asleep. You'll sleep a bit less but feel a lot more rested.

As a rule, far more can be accomplished in a calm and relaxed manner. Then your mind is free to concentrate on what you are doing, without being distracted.

Once Reb Chaim of Tsanz visited Reb Eliezer of Zhikov. Before the morning prayers, he engaged Reb Eliezer in a profound and brilliant intellectual debate on a halachic matter. When he went to pray, however, he concentrated with soul-stirring intensity. He was asked how he managed to engage in intense intellectual activity one minute and soulful davening the next.

He explained, "When I begin to pray, I forget that there is such a thing in the world as Torah study, and when I am engaged in Torah study, I forget that there is anything in the world apart from Torah study."

If we are totally *with* and *in* what we are doing, we will experience longer and longer stress-free periods throughout our day.

A person who davens three times a day and sets aside specific times for learning Torah, and he truly "enters" these times and removes everything else from his mind, will see a side benefit of reduced stress. These times can be like drinking from a refreshing, rejuvenating stream.

Where was the Torah given? In the Sinai desert, a barren and desolate corner of the earth, without human, animal, or plant life. God chose a place empty of all distractions, pleasures, demands, or worries. In the same way, we can receive the Torah during our set times for learning without allowing any outside matters intrude. When we learn, for that period of time nothing else exists but the Torah. We immerse ourselves in Torah and become refreshed and strengthened by it.

Your creativity and effectiveness will increase considerably if you concentrate totally on whatever you are doing, freeing your mind from other distractions. When you are eating, focus on eating; when you are going to sleep, focus on going to sleep. In this way you can learn to relax and enjoy whatever you are doing, whether it is household tasks or complex mathematical calculations, whether you are in the office or at home. There are certain duties we all have to perform, so we might as well enjoy them and become involved in the present as we are doing them.

It could be that you have some issue or situation in your life which causes you so much stress that you feel it is constantly with you. You just can't put it out of your mind.

Imagine that you owe your bank five thousand dollars. That debt goes everywhere with you, spoiling everything you do. When you go to work, your debt goes with you, so that you have difficulty concentrating. When you eat, you can't enjoy your food, because the bank manager is sitting beside you in your mind, saying, "How can you enjoy your food when you owe the bank five thousand dollars and you don't know how you're going to pay it back?" You go for a walk and the debt goes with you; you read a book and it stares up at you from the page.

What you have to do is consciously take the bank manager and the debt and the bank statements out of ninety percent of your day and allot them a half-hour a day. During this half-hour you can think and worry and consider what you will do about it. But after that half-hour is over, you must put it out of your mind until the next day. If it intrudes, make a short note to remember what you thought of so you can deal with it during the next day's half-hour.

With this method, the bank manager won't be able to spoil your ice cream sundae or interfere with your business meeting or hover while you read the paper.

Stress and Judaism

A study at Tel HaShomer Hospital in 1971 showed that Jews who pray daily in the synagogue suffer less from heart disease than those who pray occasionally or not at all. They divided their subjects into three groups:

1. those who daven in shul every day,

2. those who daven occasionally or seldom, and

3. those who never daven.

In the first group the number of those who had heart attacks during a period of five years were 29 out of 1,000. In the second group, the number was 37 out of 1,000. And in the third group the number was 56 out of 1,000. This number was almost double that of the religious group. (It should be noted that these figures came from a study made in a government hospital by secular researchers.)

Similar studies have been done over the years with similar results. One study done in 1993 at Tel Aviv University evaluated over ten thousand men in Israel and found that Torah observance provided a large degree of immunity to coronary heart disease.

Aside from set times for prayer and study, Jews have another powerful built-in stress-breaker: the day of Shabbos. This day transports us into another dimension where mundane matters are put aside.

Shabbos is a day where even the most guilt-ridden workaholic has to stop what he is doing for twenty-five hours. He is obliged to alter his thinking patterns during that time — and since this is the halachic requirement he need not feel guilty for relaxing.

People who have started keeping Shabbos are amazed at

the increase in their general energy level and the dividends in efficiency and creativity. Many find a marked improvement in their general health.

When you observe Shabbos you have a complete break every seven days. All your attention is taken up with matters completely different from those of the week. You are divorced from the world of business and can now spend time in spiritual and emotional growth and healing. It is as if you are taking a spaceship and going on a twenty-five-hour trip to another world, coming back rejuvenated and energized.

Shabbos also puts life back into perspective, with the tangible awareness that we are living in God's world and can put our trust in Him completely. By not creating on Shabbos ourselves we remember Who is the true Creator and Who is in charge. We come to realize that we are not swimming in a sea of meaninglessness.

Chapter 5

Burnout

This snake looks somewhat black and sooty. He leans on the ladder at his side, listless and apathetic. We have all heard of burnout, when inspiration and energy seem to drain away and we are left feeling empty and unable to function.

> Continued stress can deplete the body's resources and lead to chronic fatigue, loss of appetite, or overeating and other reactions. Coping ability may diminish, causing feelings of insecurity and inadequacy, and even depression. At the same time, the body's immune system becomes disrupted, increasing the chance of illness.
>
> *(Healthnet 1997)*

What may lead to burnout is if you perceive your work (or your life) as stressful and beyond your ability to cope. It is the *perception* (or misperception) that is the key.

Many people work extremely hard and burn the candle at both ends, yet they do not burn out. In and of themselves, hard work and insufficient rest seldom lead to burnout. Some people even thrive on such a regime. These are often the people who see every aspect of their work as profoundly meaningful. For example, many great rabbis and *rebbetzins* work from morning till night helping their fellow Jews. Rather than burning out they are energized by the importance of their work.

What Is Burnout?

Burnout is not something which appears suddenly. The subtle negative changes that erode a person's internal and external world come slowly and often go unnoticed.

> Burnout typically manifests itself as a combination of physical, mental, and emotional exhaustion, loss of commitment, disengagement from one's work, and a general inefficiency in adapting to the unique demands of one's relationship with the environment that surrounds the delivery of human services.
>
> *(Thomas Muldary, Burnout and Health Professionals: Manifestation and Management [Norwalk, Conn.: Appleton-Century-Crofts, 1983])*

A person feels no energy or inspiration. His enthusiasm is replaced by feelings of hostility, resentment, and frustration. He feels used up and unable to give to his family, his friends, and his work and sees no way to rectify this situation. He begins to cut himself off emotionally.

Symptoms can be in the realm of mental exhaustion, which can affect a person's attention, concentration, and problem-solving ability. He can also experience negative changes in his attitude toward others.

There is also a general free-floating anxiety. The person feels emotionally depleted and at the same time irritable and nervous. There is a pervasive sense of discouragement and emptiness, a sense of needing every bit of energy one has to get through the day.

Burnout in the work situation can be caused by unsurmounted, prolonged occupational stress. In certain occupations there are specific stresses which undermine a person's functioning. A teacher who faces a class that is too large, a workload that is too heavy or that is not within her field of training, or a situation where she cannot give her best feels her efficiency and satisfaction slipping away. She becomes aware that she is losing control of the class. She is not teaching in a way that the children can absorb the lesson, and she has a reduced sense of accomplishment on all levels. She becomes angry and resentful toward herself and her students. As the teacher loses her inspiration, the children become bored and misbehave. A bitter, vicious cycle ensues.

Lack of appreciation from people who are significant to us can also lead to burnout. A wife whose husband never expresses appreciation for her cooking, her handling of their children, or her housekeeping skills can become disheartened and insecure. The most excellent cook might lose heart if no one ever compliments her food or eats it with any enthusiasm. She may decide that no one really cares anyway, so why should she bother, and this attitude begins to pervade all areas of her life.

The mother of young children might experience chronic sleep deprivation and feel continuously tired and stressed. She might cease to care for her own needs. She stops taking an interest in her appearance and feels more and more apathetic, unwanted, unappreciated, unloved, exhausted, and worthless.

In short, emotional exhaustion and burnout can come in any situation where there is a heavy workload, lack of appreciation or success, and difficult working or living conditions — especially where there is no hope of change.

But what can be done about this? Where is the ladder that leads out of this bleak situation?

Are there any ladders? Are there any ways out?

Of course there are ways out. The very idea that there might not be is part of the despair and hopelessness so characteristic of burnout.

Overcoming Burnout

First, you must realize that you are experiencing burnout. You must acknowledge that the problem exists.

The next step is to make a genuine and serious commitment to do something about it.

Now you must take action to bring about real, positive changes in your life. Look at yourself and take an inventory of your life. Be honest about both the positives and the negatives. Often people see only the less desirable traits within themselves. To make a true inventory you must also see what is positive so you can build on it.

While doing inventory you might become overwhelmed by your discovery. Therefore it's important to break these issues down into manageable bits which you can work on. For example, if your home has become a mess, you can begin by sorting out one shelf or one drawer or one room at a time. Or if you're a teacher and have a very large class, picture each child as an individual and give thought to his or her needs.

It is important to start with the simplest tasks, whether at work or at home. Sometimes people even give up on the simple things due to their sense of everything being unmanageable.

Communication with others and gaining their cooperation are vital factors to combating burnout. When we feel we are losing control, we tend to cut ourselves off. But now we need our friends more than ever. We must work on building mutual trust so we can share our fears and feelings.

If you are in a position where your workload — whether inside or outside the home — is truly impossible to cope with you must acknowledge this and communicate this to others. See if something can be done on a practical level to reduce your work. You may have to discuss with your employers how your talents and potential can be better used so you are not asked to do work you feel you are not cut out for.

When asking for work more suited to your abilities, you must be honest with yourself. You must face your weak points along with your strong points. You may have to reappraise your goals. It is important that your work be both realistically suited to you as well as meaningful for you.

You must develop trust and a sense of confidence both in yourself and in others and a sense of optimism that something can be done to improve your situation.

Here again it is important to break things down into manageable parts. If you have been taking on too much responsibility, you must try to do what you can to the best of your ability and let others do the rest. Accept the fact that you cannot do everything. Often burnout decreases your ability to function until you cannot even cope with what you were always capable of doing. Or there may be changes in your life, like a new baby or an ill parent, that force you to re-assess your responsibilities. Delegate some of these respon-sibilities until you feel on top of things again.

Developing a sense of humor can help a great deal. You may have to change your attitude and learn to laugh at your own blunders.

It is important to distinguish between home and work to keep a balance between energy for work and energy for home. Never allow yourself to become exhausted by either. Sometimes it helps to begin your day twice, once as you pre-pare for work and once as you prepare to go home. I spoke to a very busy doctor who told me that in this way she could be fresh for her family rather than feel wilted from having been with patients for three-quarters of the day.

Some of us tend to overwhelm ourselves with work that exhausts us, especially if a tendency toward perfectionism traps us into taking on more than is reasonably expected. It is imperative to work out a program within what is expected and what we really can achieve.

Time management is vital. In this way you can control your time instead of letting it run away from you. You need to organize time for yourself when you can collect your thoughts and return revitalized. It does not have to be more than ten minutes a day.

Appreciating yourself and your work can lift you up from low self-esteem and burnout, but many worry that high self-esteem will cause them to lose their humility. This is not the case. A person with low self-esteem becomes absorbed in his own misery and focuses excessively on himself. The truly humble person reaches outside himself to others and is not at all self-absorbed.

There is no problem in recognizing the value of your efforts and the positive results you are achieving. It can only spur you on to greater fulfillment in a happy, relaxed way.

Spiritual Burnout

I have identified another form of burnout which I call "spiritual burnout," where the person's sensitivities seem to have grown dull.

The truth is that the soul can never "burn out." This is a feeling rather than a fact — a person feels he is no longer in touch with his spiritual side. It's as if all inspiration has gone and Hashem seems far away. Davening becomes meaningless. Learning, dry and tasteless. Mitzvos are carried out in a mechanical way. You may feel unable to give, teach, or inspire, unable to impart to others the beauty of *Yiddishkeit*. Everything has become humdrum, tedious, and routine.

If you had even the remotest idea how much your davening and your actions mean to Hashem, you might see things differently. It is important to think about this. It is too easy to feel unappreciated and that your actions are meaningless.

Of course you know that Hashem commanded us to do these things, and so you continue to do them. But you may feel abandoned, as if the Commander gave commands and then left us on our own to carry them out.

The first paragraph in the Shema is written in the singular. It is speaking to you as an individual, and it tells you to love Hashem with everything you've got. Think about that and you will start to appreciate the value of a mitzvah. It comes from Hashem. It is Hashem's will. By doing it we bind ourselves to Hashem. The commandment is the glue that attaches the Commander to the one who was commanded. That means you and me.

We may feel discouraged. We don't see the Redemption. We don't see the Beis HaMikdash being rebuilt. But we must "raise our eyes Heavenward and contemplate the work of the Creator." Then we must look at ourselves and appreciate the wonders of our own Creation.

A book I always enjoy reading is Rabbi Avraham's Katz's *Designer World*. He has a brilliant way of portraying the wonders of nature and the human body in the most inspiring way. It is hard to remain unmoved when reading such a book.

The *yetzer hara* uses certain psychological traps to interfere with your service of Hashem. These traps can cool down your enthusiasm, block your emotions, and, in the extreme, cause spiritual burnout. By looking at and working with these traps we can find ways to emerge refreshed and with renewed inspiration.

The first trap plays on low self-esteem. If the *yetzer hara* can convince you you're not important, you surely won't see your davening as important. An honest rethinking of the value of each word of Torah and davening uttered by a Jew — any Jew — may bring back enthusiasm and warmth.

Another trap the *yetzer hara* uses is to keep us rushing and unable to relax. We daven at a tremendous speed and our message is, strangely enough, "Please, Hashem, don't bother me. I am busy davening. Don't interrupt me with feelings of love or devotion or closeness to You. I have to get this davening over with." Now, although this might sound totally absurd, it has more than a ring of truth.

As I mentioned before, it's important to try to live in the

here and now, not ten minutes ahead of yourself, your mind always on what you have to do next. Living ahead of yourself means that while you are davening you're thinking about what to eat for breakfast. While you are eating breakfast you think about the drive to work. On the way to work you are picturing what's going on at work.

People have to learn to stop and *be* exactly where they are. When you are eating, eat; when you're davening, daven. In this way time will slow down and not rush past irretrievably. In fact, you will find you have more time than you ever imagined.

I often work with groups of medical students, and invariably they ask how to convey caring and interest to a patient when they only have about seven minutes with him. I tell them that instead of arriving in a rush and being tense for the whole seven minutes, they should relax, "glue their feet to the floor," and be with the patient, speaking slowly so the patient feels a sense of timelessness. Then they can move calmly to the next patient and give him the same undivided attention.

You know how much time it takes you to daven. You can devote exactly the same amount of time or, if you wish, add another five or ten minutes, and close off that time so that nothing else matters or exists. The difference is incredible.

Another way the *yetzer hara* chills our feelings for *Yiddishkeit* is by making us feel that Hashem is far away. You daven, but as far as feelings go you could be reading the telephone directory in a foreign language. It is, of course, impossible for Hashem to be far away because Hashem is everywhere. Hashem is real and present and listening. It is only our *feelings* that make us feel Hashem is far away, but that is our own, erroneous perception, totally unrelated to fact. Hashem is closer than we can ever imagine, closer to us than we are ourselves.

Another trap which distances us from Hashem is feelings of guilt. A healthy acknowledgment of guilt will lead one to do *teshuvah* and this is positive. But after we have done *teshuvah* and changed our actions, are we still davening halfheartedly, because "how could Hashem want to be close to me after that?" This residual feeling of guilt and worthlessness must be replaced with a belief in Hashem's loving forgiveness.

And, of course, anger is one of the *yetzer hara*'s favorite weapons. It takes its toll on us in every way and poisons our days. We have to confront it and let it go.

The last thing I will mention is the nonpathological experience of depression. Depression can bring a person down to greater depths than any sin can. With depression comes doubt (another of the *yetzer hara*'s favorites) and despair and a clouding of *emunah* and *bitachon*. This is something a person can fight and must fight. Being happy is a discipline, just as loving one's husband or wife is a discipline, just as loving Hashem is a discipline. It is a discipline of the mind and heart and is well within your reach. You don't have to think depressing thoughts. You don't have to be sucked into the morass of self-pity and disillusionment. You don't have to feel that the pseudo-reality of the physical world is the ultimate reality and thus give in to despair.

Recognizing these traps when the *yetzer hara* lays them at your feet will enable you to stand strong and not fall prey to spiritual burnout.

Chapter 6

STRESS AND TENSION WITHIN THE HOME

Picture a snake curled around your house, squeezing all the inhabitants in its grip. This is the atmosphere that has been created in some homes.

Other homes are like a country garden where each family member is a flower of a different color growing freely at its own pace.

Clearly it is not the interior decorator who creates the atmosphere in the home. Nor does the atmosphere depend on whether a family is rich or poor. The poorest home can have a warm, homey atmosphere which cheers up all who enter. Creating and maintaining a positive atmosphere in the home requires work, and every member of the household contributes to it.

There can be a household where the members love and care for each other deeply, and yet the level of tension can be very high. Perhaps the father is very aware of the fact that he has to leave in twenty minutes to a stressful meeting. If he communicates an atmosphere of tension, it will affect everyone around him. When he leaves to go to his meeting, all breathe a sigh of relief, though they adore and respect him.

Perhaps it's the wife and mother causing stress. Her husband comes home, and his loving but oversensitive wife is in a state of tension over a disagreement with a neighbor. This makes him feel uneasy. The atmosphere is heavy and unpleasant. If this becomes a common occurrence, he will find himself coming home later and later without even realizing it consciously.

It may be the children who are increasing the tension to an uncomfortable level. A teenage girl may pull her younger sister's hair to start an uproar so she can be entertained while doing difficult and boring homework.

There has to be a commitment to work on the atmosphere in the home, a commitment to constantly diffuse and reduce the tension. Tension can pile up just like dirty laundry and needs to be dealt with regularly.

Let's go back to the husband in the first example. He could help matters by viewing his short time at home in a different way. He could say to himself, *I can be home for twenty minutes before I have to go to the meeting. During this time I will try to truly be there and focus on my family. This will help me relax and also benefit my wife and children.* With this attitude, time will suddenly seem to slow down. Even if he has to eat quickly, it doesn't have to be done in a tense way. Those twenty minutes at home can refresh and restore.

The wife we mentioned could also work on the atmosphere in her home. She could make an effort to put her emotions on the back burner and be relaxed when her husband and children come home later.

At the same time, the man of the house should not think that if he has been at the office or *kollel* and his wife has been home all day that she has been doing absolutely nothing. He must recognize that keeping house, cooking, shopping, and looking after children is hard work. As it is important for the wife to prepare for her husband to come home, it is equally important for him to prepare to greet her with care and concern.

If you usually come home grouchy, grunt a "hello," and make a beeline for the couch and the newspaper, it's time to try a new approach. Make a point of greeting everyone in the household, show an interest in what everyone is doing, and then withdraw with the paper. This will change the atmosphere considerably and, in fact, takes very little effort. Often it is necessary to begin the day twice — once in the morning before work and the second time after work, when you come home.

Children and teenagers can also decide to help create a good atmosphere. They need to understand that, as part of the family, they must contribute to the harmony of the home. Most teenagers are aware of their potential influence in the home. There is often no one as effective in calming down a younger sister or brother. Encourage your children to help each other. Tell them, "Your contribution can make a very big difference. If you didn't realize it before, try it and you'll see."

Ideally the home should provide a haven of security from which family members gain the strength to face their daily tasks. A tension-free atmosphere is a matter of choice. Why so often do we not choose it?

Self-Esteem in the Home

Another critical factor in maintaining a positive home atmosphere is the development of a good sense of self-esteem among family members. The family can build up and enhance its members' self-esteem or break it down to painful levels. Building self-esteem should be one of the central goals of parents, as it is crucial for each child to think well of himself.

Since children crave parents' approval and respect, it is important to be free with praise. Children need encouragement, to be assured they are capable of doing the tasks set out for them, and, of course, to be given tasks that are within their range of capability.

Parents should make a habit of pointing out what the child does well. They should not worry that this will inflate a child's ego. He needs to have a sense of his capabilities to withstand the challenges he'll encounter in school — in life.

To promote self-esteem we should create an atmosphere of respect and love in the home, giving a child the time and freedom to be himself and express himself. When a child feels secure, all his natural good attributes flourish. When he has respect for himself he can more easily respect others. When he likes himself he will find it easier to like others. A child who feels he is not cared for can become unhappy and aggressive. His poor self-esteem becomes poorer, and he feels unwanted, unattractive, humiliated, and unsuccessful. A child who feels he somehow doesn't belong to those who are important to him may suffer great anxiety and pain and spend all his time and energy struggling to secure a place.

To gain acceptance a child may become more cooperative and helpful, but more likely he will become noncooperative and destructive. His parents will respond by paying a lot of attention to his destructive efforts, making his negative actions more worthwhile than his constructive ones.

Some of the things children do to gain attention can cause a great deal of tension. They may make faces, talk loudly, tell shocking stories, or continually ask questions. They may purposely play deaf or leave things around for others to pick up or trip over. They may kick their siblings or pull hair.

When parents respond with irritation it makes matters worse. Many hours are wasted in the resulting chaos. A child who feels hurt may do all sorts of things to hurt back. He may destroy property, steal, strike others, or say things like "I hate you." The worst way the parents can react is to try to hurt back or, on the other hand, to feel guilty. It is important not to engage in battle or to show hurt or guilt in voice, word, or facial expression. This just reinforces the behavior we so want to get rid of.

It is important to have positive interactions with the child at a time when he is not demanding destructive involvement or trying to defeat or hurt the parent. It is important to relate to him in a warm, accepting manner, especially when he is trying to behave in a constructive manner.

It is essential to foster an atmosphere of mutual respect where the rights of each child and parent are ensured, where all ideas and opinions are considered (though not necessarily accepted). And when we don't accept a family member's idea we should make a point of explaining why.

Respect the child's personality. Although he is immature, the child possesses all the emotions and sensitivities of his elders. Parents should not insult their children or embarrass them before others, and their confidences should be held in trust. I know many people who lost trust in their parents at an early age when they realized their parents discussed their confidences with friends, at times even laughing about them. Mutual respect is irreplaceable and so easy to achieve.

All parents must deal with the problem of children fighting. Children fight among themselves, and this should be handled in a way in which the rights of all, both parents and children, are respected.

When fighting, children should be treated as a group rather than as individuals. A parent who tries to be judge, jury, and executioner when children fight puts himself in an impossible situation. The parents may fall into a pattern of automatically siding with the youngest or weakest. Whatever the parent decides, some of the children will claim the judgment is unfair.

Parental intervention also prevents children from learning the art of resolving conflicts and inspires them to fight even more to test their parents' love. Each child sees proof of his parents' love in the fact that they sided with him.

Another important factor is that many children quickly learn to stage more fights to keep their parents involved with them. Parents would be wise to say such things as "Reuven, this is between you and Danny. I know you two can work it out."

When a child becomes angry, he often finds himself saying and doing things he regrets. He has become a victim of his own anger and must struggle to regain self-control. However, if the child can provoke his parent to lose his temper, he will feel he has won a certain mastery of the situation.

Therefore by remaining firm and not flying into a rage a parent maintains control and models for his child the healthy response to provocation.

Discipline is an essential part of guiding a child, but it is important that punishment be followed by love and that it not be taken as a rejection of the child himself, but rather as a dissatisfaction with the act he had committed.

Teenagers can bring a great deal of tension into the home. It is important for the adolescent to be able to speak his mind and express his hostility without the parents becoming angry. However, he must understand that he cannot spew forth his venom at will. Rather, he must use good manners and consider the appropriateness of every situation. He can say how he feels with respect for the feelings of others. It is important not to push for intimacy with adolescents. They will confide in you when they are ready. Even the most aloof child will find that there are times when he desperately wants to confide in an understanding parent.

In time the withdrawn teenager will speak, and when he does, parents should not take what he says lightly. One has to learn to read between the lines. A few words may reveal much of the turmoil the teenager is experiencing.

An adolescent's destructive behavior is often a cry for help rather than an effort to hurt or embarrass other family members. He may need even greater trust and closeness than he did as a child. It is advisable never to give advice in the midst of an adolescent's emotional storm.

A good parent-child relationship should help minimize natural adolescent rebelliousness. Parents should always remember that no matter how much the adolescent protests to the contrary, he needs them desperately.

When Disharmony Strikes

The atmosphere in the home can be worked on until it becomes a haven for the whole family. Each has to play his or her part in reducing the tension, fostering mutual respect and giving one another the space to grow.

However, there are times when there is no alternative but to end a marriage, and therefore it is important to discuss some of the effects of divorce on children.

Families define who we are and where we belong within the larger social framework. When divorce strikes, there is a confusion of identity for all concerned — husband, wife, and children. There is also a confusion of ethical standards, and the child's natural ongoing imitation of the parents' ethics and morals is disrupted. The child's world is broken and this affects children of any age.

It is obvious that divorce has devastating effects on the adults concerned. There is often a marked drop in self-esteem. There is loneliness exacerbated by the loss of old friends who take sides. There is often the loss of connection with one's children. There is often an increase in financial difficulties and the knowledge that one has to start over.

It will take an added effort when dealing with all this to be of support and comfort to the children. Both the parent who is awarded custody and the one who will see the children on visits must strive to put aside his own emotional turmoil enough to be available to his children. Every effort should be made to maintain peaceful relations for the sake of the children. To bad-mouth the other spouse or ask a child to take sides is highly irresponsible parenting and can destroy a child's natural love and trust of his parent. This can cause grievous harm in the years to come.

Shalom Bayis

Tension between a couple can be caused by the littlest things. For example, some people insist on being irritable before they've had their morning cup of coffee. This ruins every morning in many families. What could be the best part of the day, a send-off with enthusiasm, is instead a miserable, hostile time. The irritable person does not realize this attitude is well within his power to change.

The children go off to school grumpy, the husband rushes off to work with acid indigestion, and the mother feels let down because someone decided that "I am not a morning person." He is blaming his faults on his nature instead of seeing that he has formed his nature around his faults. He or she is saying, "That's the way I am. Don't try to change me."

No one *has* to be a grouch — before his morning coffee or at any time. He has a choice.

A person does not have to be at the mercy of his moods. Barring specific medical conditions, such as postpartum depression or hormonal imbalance, moody people are those who self-indulgently allow themselves to be so.

There are men who drive themselves relentlessly, walking around like emotional time bombs ready to explode, making themselves prime candidates for all kinds of illnesses such as heart attacks, strokes, and ulcers.

The wife can do much to relieve the tension and make her home into a haven. She should be sparing with criticism. In a good relationship, constructive criticism can be invaluable, but timing is important. It is best to discuss issues when the other person has had the opportunity to rest and regain his physical and emotional strength and energy. And, of course, no criticism should be expressed vindictively.

It is important not to nag. Nagging destroys morale and produces fatigue in all concerned. If someone has failed at something, you should never say, "I told you it wouldn't work." Instead you can help him rationally appraise what went wrong. You can make it clear that your love and acceptance are not based on the other's material success but on his human worth. Express appreciation. Help him enjoy the children and relax with them and not have to be the sole giver of punishment. Wise are those who make their home a place of comfort and relaxation and not a museum or showpiece for others. In such an environment, family members can gain the strength to deal with the pressures of the outside world. Frustration at home following frustration at work is a bitter thing to endure.

Whoever works outside the home should be allowed to come in and catch his breath before being confronted with household problems and chores. It is difficult to view your home as a haven if every time you enter you are immediately confronted with broken appliances, family problems, and bad news. Family members should learn to be good listeners, encouraging others to share their responsibilities, struggles, and daily burdens.

It is important that couples make an effort to communicate and to set aside time to really talk. Burying themselves in the newspaper day after day is not going to build a relationship. People who avoid conversation are only punishing one another. Some men feel their wives don't really care or listen to what they have to say. Or they are afraid of an emotional outburst or cross-examination. Some women may feel their husbands don't take them seriously and talk down to them. They may therefore stop sharing the details of their daily lives.

Good communication is vital in every family. The ability to talk openly about one's deepest feelings develops in a climate of support and concern. It is important that each family member learn how to express his thoughts, wishes, feelings, and knowledge without destroying, invading, or otherwise obstructing the others.

It is very important to learn the art of listening. You may find yourself thinking about what you are going to say next rather than listening to the person speaking. Instead, practice "active listening" — try to *be* with the other person; enter his world. We can love and be devoted to our husbands, wives, and children and yet never really listen to them.

Listening to someone does not mean we must agree with him. It means we try our best to understand what the other is saying, and when he finishes we can communicate our own feelings about the matter.

A sense of humor is therapeutic in a potentially explosive situation, but sarcasm and ridicule are not healthy expressions of humor because they devalue the other person. We can laugh with, but we should never laugh at.

Brothers and sisters can truly be best friends. But without communication and an active commitment to reduce tension, that closeness is very difficult to bring about. I have seen more than one tension-filled home where the husband and wife feel that the love between them is dead. I have asked them to practice tension-reducing methods and to work on improving the atmosphere of the home to make it emotionally pleasant. Suddenly they find their love blossoming once more and flowering in this new environment.

If each family member works at being positive and not getting offended at every little thing, the atmosphere at home will improve dramatically. Working on family relationships brings indescribable rewards to all. Just as we tidy up our home every day, so we should not go to sleep at night without airing our feelings and making peace with one another.

One of the built-in hazards of marriage is monotony — over the years relationships can become humdrum, dull, routine. At the same time, the glamour of the outside world seems to outshine the excitement of marriage. The psychologically brilliant Torah laws of family purity of separation and togetherness address this problem and renew the marriage constantly. In a society where so much has lost its meaning, Jewish partners are fortunate — since they may not even go near each another for almost two weeks out of every month, even a touch remains meaningful.

Another distinct advantage to Jewish family living comes with the keeping of Shabbos, a refreshing oasis and tension-shatterer. In our modern day and age, families often hurry past one another, hardly taking time to really get to know one another. Shabbos is a day when the family is together, when they sit relaxed and happy around the Shabbos table. Of course, all the family members must contribute to create and maintain a true Shabbos atmosphere.

When properly observed, Shabbos becomes a time when the mundane world is temporarily forgotten. Time stands still, and real communication can take place — for Shabbos itself is beyond and above time and can enrich and revitalize all of us.

Chapter 7

THE BLACK
DEPRESSIVE TRIP

A n ugly thick black snake runs right to the bottom of the board. This is the snake we call "depression."

Depression is part of man's nature, and we all have a certain tendency toward it. Only in the extreme is it termed pathological, but under normal circumstances there can be moments of intensely disturbing despair. Sometimes depression requires psychiatric intervention, especially if it is deep or prolonged or greatly affects sleep or appetite. In this chapter, I will refer mostly to the normal type of depression.

When someone starts the descent into depression, he may be carried along faster and faster by his own fantasies and thoughts. He may eliminate or color all that is positive in his life until he is left in total blackness.

There are various health factors that can make us feel

depressed. These can range from physical illness and hormonal changes such as birth or even flu to lack of sleep.

It is advisable to consult a doctor if the depression has lasted longer than two weeks and patterns of sleep or appetite change. Other red lights are loss of energy, anxiety, poor concentration, prominent guilt feelings, and suicidal thoughts. It is even more imperative to seek help if there was a previous depressive episode or a family history of depression.

When one becomes depressed, it is like boarding a train speeding through a tunnel with increasing degrees of blackness as it races past stations toward a deep pit of destructive and negative thoughts.

I have asked people to tell me what happens on that train. One typical train ride might go something like this:

> My best friend has hurt me again. She said she can't meet me for lunch, and I know she meant she's tired of me. I can't bear it. Everyone hurts me. I don't have any friends. People think they're my friends, but I'm sure they don't really care about me. They only want to be my friend for what they can get out of me. Or perhaps they pity me. Well, I don't want to be pitied. Maybe I shouldn't even be around.
>
> I remember that Ettie said something last week that I didn't pay attention to at the time, but I see now that she meant I was a nuisance, a drag. I'm sure that's what she meant.
>
> I look awful. I've put on so much weight. I'll never get it off.
>
> Exams are soon — I know I'm going to fail. I've done well in the past, but I can't do any better. I won't

achieve anything — I'm no good. I have no right to be alive. Maybe I should just die. Who would care? Even Hashem seems to have disappeared. If Hashem doesn't care, why should I care?

It is important to note the stations or stopping points on the black train ride. We must learn to take advantage of them, to deliberately "get off" this train, to derail this train of thought and busy ourselves with something else — anything else — until we pull out of this trap. If we knew how poisonous and dangerous this snake is, we wouldn't let him get close to us. We wouldn't feed him and encourage him along the way. We would run away as fast as possible.

Depression can bring a person to horrifying places where he loses his sense of responsibility because "nothing matters anymore." People can allow things to happen which they would not even consider when they are in a more positive frame of mind. Depression can lead to drug and alcohol abuse and all kinds of disturbed and immoral behavior because he has "given up, so what's the difference?"

Some types of depression have to be treated with an antidepressant or other medication. This is, however, very much the exception rather than the rule, and we can usually overcome depression either by ourselves or with the help of a friend or professional counselor, depending on the complexity of the situation.

Here I would refer once again to the ten cognitive distortions and the ways to untwist them described in chapter 2. This has been remarkably effective in combating depression. As with many other things, depression has both negative and positive aspects. In fact, the nonpsychiatric depression can be placed loosely under two types: the positive, or motivating, constructive depression and the negative, demotivating, destructive depression.

Destructive depression incapacitates you. It can make you unable to perform simple daily tasks. Mothers neglect their children. Employees neglect their work. They become careless and self-involved and may wallow in their feelings of hopelessness, misery, and self-pity, hanging on to and encouraging these emotions.

When someone is depressed, Hashem feels far away. The person may have difficulty davening with any enthusiasm, and everything will seem bland and lacking inspiration.

Constructive depression is a totally different experience. It springs from an awareness of shortcomings but includes a positive determination to overcome these failings. It is a transitory state that leaves the person feeling active and alive.

One must beware not to sink from a positive depression into a negative one. Depression comes to all of us at one time or another, and there is often an initial point when we can still decide whether to accept it as a positive or a negative experience, whether to use it to grow or to despair.

To turn this snake into a ladder, you must make an honest assessment of the real situation and a conscious decision to fight the depression — though it may be a fierce fight.

If you have already developed the habit of focusing on the down side of life, you must break this tendency with a conscious effort of will. Becoming positive and remaining positive is a discipline to be worked on.

Once, at the supermarket, I took a shopping cart which had something wrong with the wheels and it kept on veering off to the left. It took all my energy to control it, especially as it became fuller and heavier. In the same way, some of us have to struggle constantly to remain positive.

Batya is an extremely attractive woman. She has a handsome, wealthy husband, a luxurious house, and two lovely, intelligent children.

As she'd sit crying in my office I'd watch the tears splash from her face past the exquisite diamond rings on her fingers.

Batya was a person who seemed to have everything. She had been to psychiatrists and had experienced various medications and other treatments, but she remained negative, depressed, and unable to function as a wife or mother.

I also tried almost every kind of therapy, but I, too, had failed. Then one day she said she had decided to "end it all."

I asked her why and she replied: "How can I carry on living? Everyone has failed to help me. Tell me one person who could make me better!"

"I KNOW THE PERSON WHO CAN MAKE YOU BETTER."

Batya looked at me in surprise.

"IT'S YOU!"

Batya was startled. For the first time she was able to understand and to take control of her own therapy. And she was successful.

I think all of us working in the field of psychotherapy and counseling have had patients who've been from doctor to doctor and have resisted all efforts to heal them. They have been analyzed, conditioned, medicated, and sometimes even given electric shock treatment, all unsuccessfully. Then they disappear from the psychiatric scene and emerge after a year or two, confident and coping. They usually say they decided to get better by themselves, and they often succeed beyond belief. No one can help a passive recipient of therapy. However, once a person decides on his own to overcome his depression he will become well and his true self will emerge.

This, of course, is not true of a depression that is biochemical in origin. In these instances it cannot be overcome solely through an effort of will (although even in this case the will can help considerably).

Interestingly, even when we are feeling down in the dumps we are usually quite capable of dealing with *other people's* problems in a positive manner. How many times have you heard, "If anyone came to me with the same problem, I would be able to help him and advise him. But now that I have this problem, I just can't help myself." Taking an extreme example, a person may feel wretched, inadequate, and even suicidal — and yet, if he would be totally honest, he would admit that not all of him feels suicidal and only part of him wants to die.

If a person is thinking of suicide he has the power to combat this drive within himself. His other self or positive side can apply the brakes and pull him back to his senses. If he has been neglecting his health, not eating or caring for his bodily needs, he should view his body as a friend in need. How would he care for a guest in his home? How would he cheer up a friend who is down in the dumps? Let him use the same words to cheer up his own dragging spirits.

I often say to my patients, "Get yourself to look after yourself. Get Moshe to look after Moshe!"

Chapter 8

GUILT TRIPS

You may not think guilt can be a snake. Don't we need guilt to inspire us to do *teshuvah*? Isn't guilt a ladder, albeit a difficult one? The truth is that guilt can be both a snake and a ladder.

Psychologists speak of real guilt and neurotic guilt. Real guilt would be the ladder; neurotic guilt, the snake.

Anyone taking a superficial look at Judaism might feel that it encourages guilt to an alarming degree. With 613 laws to break, with daily confession in the morning prayers, with the month of Elul and Yom Kippur focusing on repentance, surely a Jew is consumed with guilt.

In fact, the opposite is true. Judaism does not require a person to be guilty all the time. But it is a very human emotion, and there is a place for it in spiritual growth.

Just as we all experience anger, sorrow, and joy, so do we experience guilt. When are psychological problems caused? When a person has no way to relieve himself of this guilt.

A Jew has the gift of *teshuvah*. In doing *teshuvah* he faces his guilt, makes a firm resolution to change his behavior, and is released from the burden on his heart. Obviously he must make the necessary restitution for any damage or hurt he may have caused another person.

However, a person must be willing to avail himself of this wonderful gift of *teshuvah*. Many hold on to their feelings of guilt and unworthiness. They can't even daven and learn as they should. They cannot truly believe that Hashem forgives them and therefore cannot forgive themselves. This leads to neurotic guilt.

A practicing Jew has the means of dealing with guilt in a psychologically healthy way. He feels guilty as a result of doing something he should not have done or for not living up to his potential or to the expectations of the Torah. It is important for him to cherish the purity of his conscience, for repeated sinning will dull it dangerously. We are lucky to have set times of intense soul-searching, where we sift the past for things we are guilty of and in the *teshuvah* process free ourselves from them. When a person is filled with neurotic guilt it is often a cover for real, justified feelings. By pinpointing the source of our guilt and making amends or coming to terms with it, we can become truly free.

Many people condemn themselves to a life which can have no reward, no success, and no happiness. They have judged themselves for some real or imagined misdeed with a punishment much more severe than that which any other judge would mete out.

I ask these people:

"IF YOU WERE A JUDGE IN A COURT OF LAW AND SOMEONE CAME TO YOU AND TOLD YOU ALL THE

THINGS THEY HAD THOUGHT AND DONE, WOULD YOU TELL THEM THAT FROM NOW ON, FOR THE REST OF THEIR DAYS, ALL TRACES OF HAPPINESS HAVE TO BE TAKEN AWAY?"

They invariably reply, "Of course not."

"WELL, I WANT YOU TO JUDGE YOUR OWN CASE, IN A JUST MANNER, FOR TEN MINUTES EVERY DAY. YOU CAN BE VERY STRICT, BUT ONLY AS STRICT AS YOU WOULD BE ON SOMEONE ELSE. SEE HOW MUCH SUFFERING YOU WOULD REALLY METE OUT FOR YOURSELF EACH DAY."

Some therapists try to abolish guilt completely, but this is not wise. A person must face what he has done to do *teshuvah*. At times he is able to ask the person he harmed for forgiveness.

Most psychologists and psychiatrists fail to recognize the need for suffering and atonement in people who feel they have truly sinned. Professionals often feel this only serves to increase neurotic guilt; however, this is just what is needed to relieve the guilt. A therapist working to remove the concept of sin instead of letting the person work out an atonement is using an unhealthy approach and can contribute to the breakdown of the individual as well as the society he lives in.

Varda had what many people called a guilt complex. She insisted she was responsible for her grandmother's gastroenteritis attack (though she had not seen her for several days) and many other things she couldn't possibly have had anything to do with. Many sessions later, it came out that at age eighteen she stole a dress she had really wanted but couldn't afford. When the true source of her guilt was uncovered, her emotions became clear and she was able to work through what she had done.

To properly judge past guilt, it is helpful to use return trip therapy. By reliving the pivotal situation, a person can see exactly what he did and separate real and neurotic guilt. He can then acknowledge the real guilt and take steps toward rectification, eliminating the neurotic guilt that has been haunting him for years.

"My father left for *kollel* without saying goodbye to anyone. That day he was killed in a car accident.

"I could not help feeling guilty. The night before I had been naughty. I made a lot of noise and didn't put my toys away. Both of my parents were upset with me, and I felt that if I hadn't misbehaved maybe my father wouldn't have left in a temper and maybe he would still be alive today. For many years I felt I had caused his death."

Gila began to cry. Her father died when she was four, and she had carried the guilt with her for over twelve years, until at the age of sixteen she broke down in school and was no longer able to function.

As soon as Gila learned to separate her real guilt (that of annoying her parents at age four) from the neurotic guilt (that of precipitating her father's death), she began a rapid recovery.

A significant number of my patients had younger siblings who died in infancy, causing a great deal of confusion and misplaced guilt.

"I remember the cot the baby used to sleep in and my mother bending over it. I had been forgotten! Only the new baby seemed to matter.

"I became angry and bitter even at that young age, and I often wished that something would happen to make the baby go away. I would sit in the backyard and picture all kinds of magical ways to eliminate my sister.

"When she died, I felt unbelievably guilty. At the sight of that tiny white coffin, I felt I was the worst child in the world.

"Later I felt I had no right to succeed or to be really happy. If I ever began to enjoy myself, something had to come and spoil it. I must have brought disaster on myself as a way of penance."

With this kind of problem, return tripping can be particularly successful.

Each one of us has a conscience, and it is important to listen to it, but we must make sure our conscience is leading us along the path of mental health and not distorting reality. Guilt is part of the human personality, and it is an important factor in learning acceptable patterns of behavior.

How does a child learn to behave in a way that is acceptable to himself and to others? Parents teach by scolding, praising, or reacting with disapproving silence. However, this can be taken to the extreme. Parents can induce neurotic guilt the same way they can invoke real guilt. A person might have a great deal of neurotic guilt simply due to the extreme disapproval of the adults around him. Parents can induce feelings of guilt in their children especially when they tend to be perfectionistic in their demands.

Meir looked at me sheepishly and started to apologize.

"I'm sorry. I'm probably wasting your time. I don't think I really belong in a psychologist's office. I don't even know what the problem really is.

"It's just that I can't get anything done. Nothing seems to work. I feel as though I'm always doing the wrong thing, especially when it's something I really want to do. As soon as I begin to enjoy myself, I feel it's somehow wrong."

I asked Meir to tell me about his parents. He began describing his mother, dismissing his father with a casual "He doesn't count, really. He's just an extension of my mother."

His mother was an extremely dominating woman, who always seemed to know the right thing to do. Ever since Meir was young he felt he couldn't do anything without first getting his mother's approval. A person can dominate in one of two ways, either through fear or through love. His mother employed an intense mixture of both. However, it was the domination by love that had the deepest hold on him. As a child, he would do anything to gain that love, and the thought of losing it was devastating. She became his conscience. He explained that without saying a word she could cause him to feel constantly and acutely guilty.

After a few weeks of therapy Meir's mother expressed a wish to see me. With his permission I agreed, and as soon as she walked into my office I understood very clearly what he was talking about.

She was an attractive woman with a commanding, vibrant personality. One could not help liking her immediately, but after a few minutes she started making me feel guilty. it wasn't anything she actually said but a strong nonverbal message that she was perfect and I wasn't, that everything she said and did and thought was undeniably correct.

I got very little across in this session, but my insight into my patient improved markedly.

We started doing return trips to various stages of Meir's life. We met a little boy dressed in a blue velvet suit and matching *kippah* sitting on his bed crying because he had spilled orange juice over his jacket and felt he had destroyed the entire world.

We climbed a tree and met a very anxious eight-year-old Meir, proud that he had reached so high and yet feeling uneasy that his mother wouldn't approve.

We spoke to Meir before he went to yeshivah high school. He was looking forward to the experience, but felt a nagging fear that something would go wrong.

We saw him studying, playing, running, swimming, and resting. A kind of free-floating guilt pervaded his whole existence.

Even outside his home, we found he would do just about anything to avoid being in a guilt-provoking situation. As an adult, he would give in to things he did not want just to avoid the painful increase in feelings of guilt.

In many ways Meir had to unlearn the reflex of feeling guilty and make a conscious effort to rationally analyze and then dismiss these feelings. We examined guilt-provoking phrases to defuse their impact. We had to work out when feeling a healthy sense of guilt and shame were called for and when the guilt had to be "thrown out."

Therapy took a long time, but as it progressed Meir felt increasingly that he could be permitted to live without feeling he was doing something wrong.

There are times and situations in life when a person is especially vulnerable to guilt.

"I feel guilty if I relax."

"I feel guilty if I take time for myself."

"I feel guilty if I say no."

The people who say these things think this is a normal, healthy attitude.

For many women, having their first child is a great shock. A young girl who has until now been able to lead her own life, to pursue her own career, is suddenly confronted by a demanding infant who wakes her up every time she falls asleep needing food or attention. Life has changed, dramatically, excitingly, and yet in other ways horrifyingly.

Time is no longer her own, and she often switches to the opposite extreme by giving herself completely to the care of her child. She feels for some strange reason that she is not allowed to relax, to enjoy herself, to do anything for herself. Even when the baby is napping and she could rest, she feels she cannot do this. No matter how many times she is told to relax, eat a good meal, and take time for herself, she just doesn't listen.

"IF YOU SAW A FRIEND DOING THIS TO HERSELF, WHAT WOULD YOU SAY?"

"I would tell her to do something for herself — join an aerobics class or go visit a friend. I'd tell her to be sure to nap during the day."

"FINE. I WANT YOU TO SPEND TEN MINUTES IN THE MORNING AND TEN MINUTES AT NIGHT TELLING YOURSELF WHAT YOU JUST TOLD ME — AND THEN DO IT."

Guilt is positive when it helps a person do the right thing. It is destructive when it causes a person to become dysfunctional. This kind of guilt can be and must be worked through.

Chapter 9

THE VICTIM

This snake contorts itself into a very uncomfortable and somewhat resentful pose, trying not to take up anyone else's space on the game board.

Dina always carried a hurt expression. Everyone who came in contact with her felt either sorry for her or guilty or a combination of both. No one dared to not like her even though she made them exceedingly uncomfortable. People somehow felt they "owed" her though they may never have met her before. If someone criticized her in the slightest way or offered advice Dina didn't appreciate, they would quickly be cast in the role of abuser, torturer, or unfeeling monster.

They would also feel a strong sense of responsibility toward Dina, a need to solve all her difficulties and atone for the wrongs the world had inflicted on her. They would be made to feel it was a priority to satisfy her and yet be left feeling guilty afterward for not coming to her aid as quickly as possible.

If we stop to figure out why Dina and others like her take on the role of victim, we might be even more confused.

I saw a woman who told me she was being abused by her husband — he would not let her get her housework done. He had a heart condition and wanted her to sit by the bed and keep him company the entire day. In my office she was angry, tearful, and frustrated, saying she could take it no longer.

I asked her what was forcing her to spend so many hours at his bedside.

"*He* is," she almost shouted.

"WHAT WOULD HAPPEN IF YOU EXPLAINED THAT YOU COULD ONLY SIT THERE FOR FOUR OR FIVE HOURS, AND FOR THE REST OF THE DAY YOU'D BE COOKING AND CLEANING? YOU COULD EXPLAIN THAT YOU WOULD LOVE TO BE WITH HIM, BUT YOU HAVE WORK TO DO AND WILL BE NEARBY."

"He would sulk and give me the silent treatment."

Although she was feeling great resentment, this woman was allowing herself to be a victim.

I have seen men give and give to their wives until they are in serious debt. They, too, have allowed themselves to become victims. They might groan every time they sign a check, but they still sign it. An attitude of "When I say no I feel guilty" is a sure way to become a victim.

A person who can't say no can be taken advantage of by all his neighbors and friends who want him to do this or that for them. In fact, if they can't say no they may be totally overworked (but never, of course, overpaid). They never let people know they can't spare the time, and they continue to smile and speak pleasantly as they boil and bubble inside. They are victims because they let themselves be victims. I have seen countless people who protest that they can't say no either because they feel guilty or because they fear their friends will stop liking them. The victim feels that his life is ruled by others and that people take advantage of his good nature.

He must learn to say, "I would love to *but...*" I have found these words better than a simple no, which can sound harsh and unfeeling.

Learning to state your requirements and to say no is crucial to the observant Jew. If you are afraid of offending your host, you may end up compromising your standards of kashrus or Shabbos. A relative may urge you to join him at a fish restaurant, claiming you could order a kosher type of fish, but you know the entire kitchen is treif. Friends may try to convince you there's nothing wrong with coming to their party on Shabbos as long as you walk there and don't touch anything electrical. But you know they will be playing music and doing other things that are not in the spirit of the holy day. Never feel guilty to say no and stand up for your religious and moral principles. Others will only respect you more for this.

One psychologist talks about the "harried housewife," a common example of a person who can't say no.

H.H. takes on every job that comes her way and even volunteers for more. She never counters her husband's criticism and accepts all her children's demands. By midafternoon, H.H. collapses and nothing gets done. She feels she has let everyone down and berates herself without mercy.

One of the first steps in changing this cycle is for the harried woman to accept that others take advantage of her because she has taught them to do so.

An employee might start to devote every bit of spare time to his work. He arrives early and leaves late, taking work home with him. He seldom, if ever, takes a lunch break and stops socializing with others. Though bosses and co-workers will feel a little uncomfortable at first, they may find themselves piling more and more work onto the victim. The victim will become more and more angry, but this anger will not be expressed, neither by word, action, nor expression, so no one knows it's there.

The victim sees his bosses as hard and unrelenting task-masters and his fellow employees as irresponsible and possibly incapable. Life is always seen as tough. He is always harried and harassed, and it is difficult to relax in his company. It is also difficult to make jokes as he tends to take them personally.

Although you may think people like this have a lot of friends because of all they do for everyone, victims usually make others feel uncomfortable. We become uneasy when someone is totally at our beck and call, without regard for his own needs. We also think twice before asking for favors since we know we won't get an honest answer. It is also hard to reciprocate because a victim wants to keep the upper hand as the one doing for others. If you try to invite him over for a meal after he hosted you or offer babysitting help in return for help you received, you will most likely be refused. The victim has no needs or desires for himself.

Self-Pity

Closely related to being a victim is the person who is

filled with self-pity. The "poor me" attitude is a dangerous one.

Self-pity is linked to almost every chapter of this book. It is the master snake that links all the other snakes as it gathers momentum and races to the bottom of the board. A person caught up in self-pity feels sorry for himself and angry with everyone else.

The person may also feel he is the victim of his own emotions. He feels he cannot control his temper. It just overtakes him. Or perhaps he didn't study for exams because "he didn't feel like it" or "he couldn't really concentrate." He can't attend a *shiur* because he is the victim of being too tired in the evening (though there are other things for which he is perfectly awake). The person feels controlled and at the mercy of everything the *yetzer hara* puts before him. The victim says, "I can't. It's just too hard." Here again, the victim has to say no, or at least, "I would love to, *but...*" He can and must take a flying leap onto a ladder and recognize that *he* is making himself a victim and change.

Substance Abuse

We see another snake slithering down the board, a snake we might hesitate to recognize — that of alcohol and drug abuse. Most users feel they are not abusing the alcohol or drugs but that the alcohol and drugs are abusing them, forcing them to take it when they "know it is not good for them, but what can they do?" They are the "victims" of the alcohol and drugs.

Much drug dependence involves over-the-counter drugs. We take something to relieve pain, and we find it makes us feel more relaxed, so next time we are tense we take a pain reliever even though we have no pain. Soon we find that two or three work better than one, and we start to use them to "face the day."

It might be the same with alcohol. A person likes the feeling it gives him so he can express himself better. He feels less anxious and starts drinking more and more. All the time he tells himself that he is a victim.

A person seldom has to be a victim. He must emerge from the morass of self-pity and blaming others to ascend the ladder toward self-expression and assertiveness. Anyone with a problem of substance abuse should contact Alcoholics Anonymous or Narcotics Anonymous or seek professional help.

Entrapment

There is yet another kind of victim. The person who finds himself *trapped*.

Many of us have, in one way or another, at some time in our lives, felt trapped. It is almost as if we are living in a prison, locked behind bars. But these are bars of our own making. We fall into a rut and stop caring or trying.

Let us look at a few traps.

- First, let's see a real prison. John is in solitary confinement. He has no visitors and no human contact. He is not allowed to read or write. However, even in this situation, John may not be truly trapped.

- Mrs. Levi's children have all grown up and left home. She and her husband hardly speak to one another. She sits and reads novels all day long.

- Chaim works hard at the office. He then brings work home,

ignoring his family's pleas for attention. He even brings work home on weekends.

- Lisa likes bright lights and night life. She sleeps late, works in the afternoon, and goes to parties at night. She seeks friends but has only empty, meaningless relationships.

- Miri wakes up to her tranquillizers, sits in a chair most of the day taking more tranquillizers, and goes to bed with sleeping pills, one day after another after another.

It seems that these people are trapped. But it is not circumstances that have trapped them. It is their attitude to life and their way of living it. Each could make his circumstances more meaningful and more exciting.

We look forward to the day we retire and can be free, but those who have retired know that it is often the opposite of freedom. Retirement can be a prison of boredom and lack of purpose. After he retires, a person has to find something meaningful to do which will keep him challenged and fulfilled.

People who feel trapped often have a great deal of unused energy which leads to various negative patterns of thought. They need to redirect their energies into something positive, perhaps start on a new career, the more challenging the better.

Ora was an extremely attractive sixteen-year-old who had gotten involved in drugs. Her parents brought her to me because she had begun to do irresponsible things (they had no idea about the drug problem).

I did some psychological testing and found her to be of superior intelligence. Some of her tests highlighted her unconscious sense of having hurt herself.

We discussed the situation frankly, and she agreed that she didn't really want to continue with her present way of life. She applied for a program to prepare for her matriculation examination in one year. She had to work extremely hard day and night and get private tutors for extra lessons.

It took about two months of this intensive study to really notice a change in her. Her priorities changed. She was looking at lists of universities and eventually majored in social work. Her negative energy was redirected in a positive way.

To live without challenge makes us bored, tired, and depressed. Three hours spent in a dentist's waiting room can make us much more weary than three hours of performing real physical labor.

On a spiritual level a Jew might find himself trapped. As we advance along the game board our feet become entangled, and we are unable to move any further. We actually become trapped in a slavery of our own making. Instead of being embraced by the four cubits of halachah we are trapped by our own suffocating restrictions.

Low self-esteem is a trap many fall into, sometimes due to the illusion that low self-esteem means humility. In reality, low self-esteem is about concentrating on and protecting the self whereas humility is basically selfless. The snake of low self-esteem slinks feebly along the bottom of the board not wanting to get in the way or risk rejection. This type will not allow himself to succeed because he fears failing.

A person suffering from low self-esteem often has difficulty davening. Why should Hashem be interested in hearing from him? So he davens by rote, feeling that this is the only approach for a creature such as he.

We don't need to eliminate all these snakes. What we want to do is to turn them into ladders. Instead of feeling trapped as a housewife, a wife and mother can see the importance of doing dishes, laundry, child-rearing, and make it more meaningful. Retirement can be a chance to do all the things you've never done before. Climbing a ladder takes effort, but what an exhilarating challenge!

Chapter 10

*N*EGATIVE WORDS

This snake is a dangerous one. Sometimes we don't recognize him. He can look so attractive and might even imitate a ladder. He tries to convince us that he isn't really a snake, that he's just a harmless creature.

Imagine the following scenes:

A doctor sits in his office seeing patients with a calm manner and a smile on his face. The waiting room outside is packed. Suddenly the snake gives a bite and spews out poison. The scene changes. The doctor is now standing outside his empty waiting room looking up and down the street. His former patients walk past, looking away. He goes back inside and puts his head in his hands in despair.

Another scene:

A new student is being shown into a classroom. She is looking forward to being in a truly Jewish school. She is eager to learn, eager to acquire the friendship of the girls. You can tell she is not from a religious background. The snake appears again. Now the new girl is crying. She is leaving the school, never to come back, never to have a Jewish education.

We see a close and happy family around the Shabbos table. Then we see that same family torn apart by conflict, the wife and children leaving, never to return.

We see best friends deciding never again to speak to one another.

Picture a second series of scenes:

A child is lying in a hospital bed, his face chalk-white. The doctors are standing around, whispering gravely to one another. The mother and father are weeping. And then some women recite a few words from a prayer book and the child sits up and smiles. The mother and father rush over and hug him, and the doctors congratulate one another.

A young man sits gloomily at an empty table. His children are thin and pale, his wife tense and weary. A woman says some words and the scene changes. The wife and children are waving goodbye to the young man with smiles on their faces. He leaves the house carrying a briefcase, on his way to work — at last.

We see a man in jail, falsely accused, and then we see him freed by the courts after being declared innocent.

We see husbands and wives who are estranged being happily reconciled.

What was that snake whose venom poisoned all the people in the first group of scenes? That was the snake of *lashon hara*. He has the power to destroy relationships and reputations and cause terrible financial loss. He can kill at a distance, with just a few words.

And who are those women in the second group? Those are the women who say *tehillim* for others who are in trouble. Just as words of *lashon hara* are incredibly destructive, words of Torah and prayers are more powerful than we can imagine. If we had any idea what *tehillim* can achieve, we would never stop saying them.

Imagine that you are put in front of a computer and told that if you would press a certain key you would blow up half a village. Even though you could do it while sitting in the comfort of your air-conditioned room and you would not have to witness the horrendous results, you would be horrified and make a hasty exit from the room.

Words are said so quietly, so casually, perhaps over a cup of coffee or tea — words which can break up homes, erode a person's livelihood, and ruin lives. It is all done at a distance, but the wise person should keep away from it and have nothing to do with it.

There are projects where people sign up pledging not to speak *lashon hara* for one or two hours a day. This has had wonderful and far-reaching results. But at the same time, there has to be a complete rejection of any form of gossip and the awareness that we have to distance ourselves from it totally. We have to become so sensitive to this matter that speaking *lashon hara* should automatically disgust and shock us as much as if we saw someone pulling the wings off a live butterfly.

I think that the twelve steps of Alcoholics Anonymous could be applied to *lashon hara* to eradicate this tendency in people. (Rabbi Dr. Twerski discusses these steps at length in his books.)

You may protest: "But *lashon hara* isn't really so bad. The finest people do it. It isn't like eating treif or violating Shabbos, Heaven forbid!"

But in many ways it is even worse. Rambam tells us:

> Slander, one of the gravest offenses, is defined as talking disparagingly of anyone, even though it is true. According to our Sages, "there are three sins for which one is punished in this world and forfeits his portion in the World to Come. These are idolatry, immorality, and murder, but slander is equal to all three put together..."
>
> *(Hilchos De'os 7:3)*

We hold many strange beliefs about *lashon hara*. One is that it is impossible to really eliminate it from our lives. Another is that if we don't speak *lashon hara* we won't be considered "normal." Another common belief is that there is nothing seriously wrong with speaking a few bad words about someone.

If we were told that we are eating a piece of treif meat, we would spit it out immediately and lose our appetite. Unfortunately we don't have the same aversion to *lashon hara*.

Speaking *lashon hara* can be very tempting. You feel close to the person you are talking to. You feel good as you share your feelings or tell the latest news about this or that person. But the person you are talking to will feel that he can never trust you again. If you can say so many awful things about other people, what do you say when *he* turns his back?

The Alcoholic Anonymous twelve steps book says:

> Self-righteous anger can also be very enjoyable. In a perverse way we can actually take satisfaction from the fact that many people annoy us.
>
> Gossip barbed with our anger, a polite form of

murder by character assassination, has its satisfaction for us, too. Here we are not trying to help those
we criticize. We are trying to proclaim our own
righteousness.

Someone once told me, and she was being perfectly honest, that if she didn't speak *lashon hara* she wouldn't have
anything to say. All her communication skills were based on
disparaging others, and she had never developed other styles
of conversation. With a little effort she was able to explore
new subjects and styles of speech and found more joy in her
relationships.

Negative speech also includes the angry, sarcastic, or
bitter words that come to our lips, especially when we are
tense, tired, upset, or hungry. This often happens at home
and with people we love. They may react in the same way,
and this causes an ever-widening spiral of dissent.

We must realize that angry words won't make us feel good.
They don't build relationships or reinforce the self-esteem of
any member of the family — neither that of the person
speaking nor that of the person being attacked.

By watching our words, we can refrain from the negative
and begin to build on the positive. Making positive statements
has an effect both on ourselves and on others. I am not sug-
gesting that problems be shelved and not discussed, but they
can be discussed in a respectful, constructive manner. Being
careful with words and using positive language is so important that the Torah, which does not use extra words, will use a
whole phrase to avoid using a negative word.

Rabbi Yehoshua ben Levi said: "A man should never
utter an unfit word, for the Torah uses eight extra

letters in order to avoid using an ugly word, as it says, 'Of the clean beasts and of the beasts that are not clean' " (Bereishis 4:2).

(Pesachim 3)

It is so easy to use destructive words:
"You'll never be able to do that."
"I've heard all your good resolutions before."
"I hate the way you do this."
"I can't stand being around you. You really irritate me."

There may be some things that do irritate us about a certain person and that we feel would be beneficial for the person to change, but we should address those specific things rather than attack the person. Love should include a large dose of respect for the person we claim to love.

Lashon hara can cause major trauma. Probably the thing which causes parents the most heartache is when one or more of their children move away from *Yiddishkeit*, and this turn of events could have been caused by *lashon hara*.

Children and teenagers are very affected by what they hear, especially when it comes from their parents. Parents spend fortunes to see that their children are provided with a high-quality Jewish education, and yet they tear apart the very teachers into whose care they have entrusted their children and whom the children are expected to respect. These statements might not sound so bad to the adult saying them, but children see things as black and white. Even the tiniest drop of negative information can blunt the influence of a teacher or rabbi on a child. If this is repeated over and over throughout the years, our children are going to seek other role models, other people to provide them with a morality they have not found in *Yiddishkeit*.

So how can you stop gossiping and talking *lashon hara*?

First of all, you must believe that you can. No one can force you to say anything you don't want to say. Try to watch what you say one day at a time: "Just for today I won't talk *lashon hara*; I won't cut people down with my words. I will try to say something positive just for one day."

It is important to make a commitment and to be in touch with others who have made the same commitment. If two people in a group have committed themselves not to gossip, they can give each other courage. Just a look or a gentle tap on the shoulder may be enough to remind one another of this commitment.

You might say to a friend, "If you see me starting to say something I shouldn't please step on my foot. If I continue, stamp hard."

Another method is to abandon all gossip even about people in the news or people whose names you don't mention. That way you can acquire the habit of avoiding *lashon hara* completely.

A true love of our fellow Jew is the greatest barrier against speaking *lashon hara*. When real love and respect is present, negative thoughts do not even exist. By working on our love for all Jews our "need" to speak *lashon hara* will simply melt away.

Let's use our power of speech for words of Torah and prayer, which have the ability to reach the highest heavens and break all kinds of evil decrees.

Chapter 11

REGAINING AN IDENTITY

Sometimes terrible things happen that put a person's life in turmoil, and he feels unable to pick up the pieces. These are devastating losses, usually the severe illness or death of a loved one.

The despair these upheavals engender is a snake that sinks its deadly fangs into you, making you feel you can no longer go on. At this time you can't think about ladders. You can't even see the possibility of a ladder. You may feel a total collapse of your identity; you've become a stranger to yourself.

Rabbi Twerski tells the story of a man from Chelm who once visited a public bathhouse. He found himself in a terrible predicament because, without their clothes on, everyone seemed to look alike.

And if everyone looks alike, he thought worriedly, *how will I know which one is me?*

After some careful thought he tied a red string around his toe. Now he would know which person was himself by looking down at his feet. But as he got into the bath, the red string slipped off. Someone else stepped on it, and the string wrapped itself around the second person's toe. When the man saw this, he cried out in panic, "I know who *you* are, but who am I?"

Although you might not identify yourself by a red string, there are constants in everyone's life that give a person a feeling of structure and definition. They may be somebody's son or daughter, husband or wife, father or mother.

The self-esteem of many women are tied up in their husband's profession. They see themselves as the rabbi's wife or the doctor's right hand. They may also greatly rely on their high financial status. All this can change drastically after a death or divorce. The standard of living may go down forever. The woman may have to go out and find work with very little financial security if she has no training. Many women have never learned the finer details of managing finances and find themselves having to cope alone. Their entire self-image may be altered. Moshe's wife or Shmuel's wife was a totally different person from Moshe's widow or Shmuel's ex-wife.

When a man loses his wife he may be faced with responsibilities his wife had been doing. He may not be able to cook, sew, handle the shopping, or keep the apartment clean. He may feel helpless, useless, and deserted.

Many of those who have lost a person close to them find themselves asking: Who am I? What is my life all about? Do I still matter? Am I still a person in my own right?

Their conclusions, initially at least, are a resounding *NO*. No, they don't matter. They are no longer people in their own right. Their existence has ceased to have validity or meaning with the loss of the loved one.

The initial stage after a person has lost someone close to him is usually shock. The person is no longer there, and this is hard to grasp. This stage can last for months. A person may go through the death, the funeral, the *shivah*, and well into the first year and seem to be coping well. He may appear strong and not deeply affected. But then the shock wears off and devastation sets in. The person cannot function, and friends look on in surprise. "You handled it so well up to this point. Why are you so upset now?" Friends might not have time for the person now, even though they made themselves available in the first few weeks.

Anger may erupt at this stage, and the mourner becomes irritable and resentful. He may turn bitter and distance the very friends he needs. This is normal, and it is important for the mourner and his friends to be aware of it.

Depression is also normal. Some people may imagine a set timetable for mourning, but grief does not stick to schedules — the depression can persist for years. It may come in waves which totally engulf a person.

There is also often a certain hypersensitivity after a death, and this, too, can persist for years. Imagine that someone has a severe sunburn, but others are not aware of it. They come over and give the person a hug or a pat on the back, and the person screams in pain. "Don't touch me!" Traumas such as death or divorce bring with them severe emotional sunburn. Anyone who comes close will hurt the person, especially his closest friends and relatives. They will inevitably say the wrong things, because most things are the wrong things. When people realize they keep saying the wrong thing, they don't know what to say, and then they begin to avoid that person. This can lead to the mourner feeling rejected and desperate. Being aware of these pitfalls will be most beneficial both to the mourner and to his friends.

Guilt is another thing which can haunt the person. There are always questions: Did I do enough? Could I have prevented the death? Am I really allowed to make a new life?

Reconstructing an Identity

How can one turn this snake of loss of self-esteem into a ladder? How can one construct a new identity?

First you must give yourself permission to do so. You must get rid of the guilt that stops you from allowing himself to live again.

You must then redefine yourself. Do the words *widower* or *divorcée* have negative connotations? Now is the time to give new meaning to these terms.

Now take an honest look at your friends and relatives and all the people you may have withdrawn from and no longer talk to. You may have been hypersensitive and perhaps still are at times, and for this reason you pushed everyone away. It is important to explain what you've been going through and bring them close again. It is also important to seek out new friends.

At the beginning of the mourning period the mourner may have precipitated rejection and almost seemed to look for it. But now is the time to change that attitude. You don't have to refuse social invitations anymore or go to *simchahs* reluctantly and leave early. There is nothing wrong with embracing life in all its fullness and enjoying every moment.

When husbands and wives have been bereaved they may lose a sense of how important they are to their children because of their loss of self-esteem. Their sense of helplessness might blind them to the fact that they are doubly needed now by their family. Attending school plays and helping with homework must still be done, even though it may have been the other parent who handled these matters before.

The bereaved must learn to see themselves as people in their own right. They must realize that their low assessment of themselves is wrong. Their words do have value and what they do is important even if they don't feel it is so. In divorce, the parent without custody is still of great importance. He must continue to pursue the relationship even when the child shows antagonism.

It is also vital that the person not see himself as a spare wheel when in mixed company and to realize that people can relate to him as an individual. When a person works on liking himself, others will respond in kind. It is important not to see oneself as a *nebbech*.

Sometimes a person goes through a rebellious phase and questions why Hashem has done this. This, too, can be worked through, and the person can come out of it with even stronger *emunah* and *bitachon*.

Return tripping is very effective for someone who has experienced a loss. People who face traumatic situations, who have lost a parent, a spouse, a child, or a friend, are always hurt and confused, perhaps bitter and cynical. Most have not come to terms with the death or their feelings about the dead one. I take these people on return trips to the time of the illness, the hospitalization, or the death experience itself. This helps them face the situation and deal with it.

We are all equipped with a natural anesthetic. When situations become unbearable, we have a kind of "overload switch" system, and we switch off and live through these experiences as if in a dream. Our calmness usually surprises ourselves and others. This natural emotional anesthetic protects us from breaking down.

At times people become locked into this state of being emotionally switched off and remain unresponsive for months or years. During the traumatic experience this was necessary for emotional survival, but to remain in this state is harmful. The feelings must be faced and dealt with. Return trips to the traumatic experience of death or illness may overcome the bitterness, hostility, and self-pity and bring feelings of true mourning, a mourning that provides healing.

Sometimes it's beneficial to take return trips to the good times, the precious moments that were shared together. This can evoke a sense of closeness with the deceased on a deep, fundamental level.

Here is an example of one return trip a client took:

Jean was silent for a long time, so long I wondered if she would speak.

"I remember how we used to go shopping together. We didn't have much money, and we had to be careful. We always spent too much, but it was fun and we loved it.

"I remember the walks we would go on. We'd pass through the quieter streets until we reached the lake, and then we'd walk around it a few times. We had a dog, then, a Labrador who loved the water, who would always somehow get into the lake despite the cold weather. He would jump out of the lake some minutes later and shake himself dry, showering us with icy water."

Jean was crying now, but these were not the tears of bitterness of earlier sessions when she had spoken about the traumatic few months she had just endured. These tears were somehow more healing, coming straight from the heart. Whereas the other tears had brought little relief, these tears that came from remembering good things shared were a comfort.

We all carry around mental pictures of the ones we love. After a death we tend to focus on the end, the toll sickness and death took on the person's image. It is of the utmost importance to reestablish the true image of the person. Though it might be painful at first, this method has great rewards. The loved one can more easily become a part of us, and we can carry on with a more positive mental "snapshot" ready to be conjured up.

Another natural response in a person who has experienced loss is a preoccupation with the deceased, usually centered on traumatic scenes of illness and death. The person may be unable to function or concentrate because of these thoughts. It is not possible for a person to completely banish these thoughts from his mind, but it is possible to limit these thoughts to certain times when you decide to bring them up.

Another client, whose wife died in a tragic accident, struggled with this problem:

Daniel sat opposite me in extreme distress.

"I just can't get it out of my mind, not for a minute. It's with me everywhere I go. I see the accident in front of me — the way she died, the way the bricks covered her. I wonder whether she was alive and conscious for those last few seconds. What did she think about before she died?"

We talked about the accident during that session and

many others. Then we started talking about the good memories, but his preoccupation continued. Daniel's efficiency at work was affected, and he seemed to be losing his ability to function. Together we worked out a program to follow.

He'd wake up a half-hour early, make himself a cup of coffee, put on some quiet music, and for the next thirty minutes think about his deceased wife. Then Daniel would switch off the music and get ready for work, banishing from his mind all thoughts of his tragic loss. If a thought did still intrude, he would jot it down for future reference and bring his mind back to his work. During his lunch hour he could think of the accident for ten minutes only, but he had to leave the office during that time and then throw himself wholeheartedly back into his work.

At night, Daniel would set aside one hour to think about his wife and to look at her photographs. But when the hour was up, he would put her out of his mind and occupy himself with something else.

The interesting thing about this method is that Daniel was obliged to follow the set timetable and actually force himself to think of his late wife for an hour and forty minutes each day.

Also, since Daniel was unable to stop thinking about his wife's death as he went to sleep at night, I helped him think of her in more pleasant circumstances. Eventually he found real comfort, despite his pain.

This system can work in many situations where a person is plagued by disturbing and persistent thoughts.

Chapter 12

DISABILITY:
A UNIQUE OPPORTUNITY

W e have spoken at length about turning life's snakes into ladders. But some people may say, "There are certain situations that are snakes and only snakes. They could never be turned into ladders."

Indeed, there are times when it can take months, or even years, before a snake can be turned into any kind of ladder; but it can and has been done.

Perhaps one of the best examples is physical disability.

I first met Pinchas in the septic orthopedic ward. The specialist treating him realized he was depressed and asked me to speak to him.

Pinchas had been in a car accident four months previously and lay in a coma with a five percent chance of recovery. He had recovered, to the surprise of everyone, without brain damage. But his hips and legs would never function except to give off vicious spasms of pain.

Even in these difficult circumstances I was struck by the power of his personality. His sense of humor had not been affected by the intense pain which was with him at all times.

Pinchas needed to change his self-image from that of an intelligent, tough, good-looking young man to that of an intelligent, tough, good-looking young man in a wheelchair.

He had always had a vibrant personality which won him popularity and respect. But over months of having to rebuild his identity, Pinchas emerged with an unusual degree of strength, nurtured by his deeply mystical faith. He had always had a philosophical turn of mind, but his pain and desperation gave his outlook added depth.

He was discharged from the hospital, and over several years I saw him only sporadically. I was always pleased when he wheeled himself into my office unannounced, because his enthusiasm was infectious. He would tell me about the projects he was working on, about the people he was helping — and he did help them, for his natural counseling skills were enhanced by the fact that he had been there.

One day he told me he had bought a used car which he was able to drive after making certain mechanical adjustments. He said this new freedom changed his life.

When Pinchas became ill again, against all expectations, he recovered and in a very short time was driving around. Then one day he called to say he was engaged. Soon there were two wheelchairs rolling into my office as he proudly introduced Chaya, a beautiful girl with large deep-blue eyes. Her wheelchair was electric, because she was quadriplegic. She was living in a home for quadriplegics, and her fellow residents looked on in amazement as red roses and boxes of chocolates began to arrive at the door. Often they were accompanied by notes Pinchas wrote himself.

The home where Chaya lived was a place where people usually gave up on life. But here she was, with a light in her eyes, waiting excitedly for Pinchas's phone calls.

A short time later I heard that Pinchas had had a heart attack and passed away. But he had lived life to its fullest and had made a profound impression on all he came in contact with.

Chaya was devastated, but with his love for her locked securely in her heart she continued what she had been doing before, painting pictures of incredible beauty with her mouth, never forgetting the joy she had experienced.

Some of the most inspiring heroes I have known have been physically disabled or disfigured. As with Pinchas, a disabled or disfigured person has the unique opportunity to become an inspiration and motivating force for others. Someone who has "been through it" speaks with a force that is difficult to rival.

I have worked with victims of car and motorcycle accidents who had to have a limb amputated. When someone loses a limb he often goes through all the stages of mourning as he would for a death. He may become angry, depressed, apathetic, and go through alternating moods of partial acceptance and intense bitterness.

A real moment of truth arrives when he must begin to walk and fully face the anger and resentment he feels about his condition. However, in the hospital where I work, I have seen these people return from their walking lessons inspired, not only because they can envision being mobile again but because their physical therapist is someone they can admire and draw strength from. Why is this? Because this particular physical therapist has overcome a disability of his own. He is blind.

I went to see Reuven shortly after his accident. He was still on a kidney machine. His one leg was amputated below the knee, and his other leg was extensively damaged.

Reuven improved gradually during a year in the hospital, sometimes becoming extremely ill as infection raged through his body. There were moments when he would pray to die. At other times his sense of humor would triumph, and he would rock with laughter at some of the things that happened in the ward.

The time came for Reuven to start the arduous process of learning to walk. I saw him after his first lesson. Though he was exhausted and in pain, his hopes soared.

"As I was taken in my wheelchair down to the physical therapy department, I was excited to start learning to walk, but I was bitter that I couldn't just jump out of my wheelchair and start walking as I used to — all because of some driver who'd had too much to drink and had crashed into me. He got out of it without a scratch and look at me!

"By the time I got to the therapy room I was angry

and discouraged, and I felt I'd never learn to walk. Then I saw the therapist, and though he could not see the expression on my face, he seemed to have an instinctive feel about my mood and thoughts.

"I immediately forgot about myself, and my self-pity vanished. He was so gentle and understanding and yet so firm in his approach, and I thought, *If he is blind and can be such an inspiration, then I am going to be an inspiration, too.*"

Reuven improved greatly after this. The therapist always knew when Reuven had his head down while he was trying to walk. He would suddenly say, "Put your head up," and Reuven would guiltily jerk his head back. He was a constant source of inspiration to Reuven.

When Reuven left the hospital, he had found within himself the courage and determination he had seen in the therapist. And so, in a certain sense, a disability became an asset, for if the therapist had not been blind, his effect on his patients would have been much less.

There is a terrifying neurological disease called Guillain-Barré syndrome. Over a matter of days, even hours, a person becomes progressively paralyzed until even the muscles for breathing shut down. In extreme cases, the person must be put in intensive care on a respirator, unable to speak or move.

I was called to see a woman in this condition who had been lying for nearly a month with no improvement. She did not have the muscle capacity to even close her eyes, and they had to be taped shut. The doctor told me that the woman was very depressed and appeared to have given up.

I remembered another patient I had seen with the same

condition. He told me of the extreme anguish he felt at not being able to move any part of his body. Despite constant re-assurance from the doctors, he doubted if he would ever move again. I remembered his joy when, a few weeks later, he was able to move one finger. A few weeks later I saw him driving himself around the hospital in a wheelchair.

When the doctor asked me to see this woman I said, "I don't blame her for being depressed. And nothing I say is going to help. I can tell her this condition will reverse itself with time, but she won't believe it."

I called the physical therapy department and asked patients who were in various stages of recovery from Guillain-Barré to come speak to her.

The patients came, some in wheelchairs, some on crutches, and they would sit by her bed and talk to her: "I also had Guillain-Barré, and I was also on a respirator. I also had my eyelids taped shut when I needed to go to sleep. I couldn't move at all. I also didn't believe this thing would ever go away, but here I am now..."

After she recovered, the woman said these visits from other patients had given her the strength to carry on and had eased her psychological pain. Nothing I would have said to her could have compared to the message of hope these people conveyed.

In the Second World War a Jewish doctor working in an army hospital would walk into the ward of wounded soldiers who had lost limbs and do a little dance from one end to the other.

Then he would stop and say, "You are wounded. You have lost limbs. Will you ever walk again? Will you ever dance like me? I can walk! I can run! I can dance!"

The soldiers were stunned at this doctor's cruelty until he dramatically lifted up his pants leg to display a wooden leg. More than anyone else, this doctor was able to get through to the soldiers and give them hope for recovery.

I have a friend named Shira who had childhood polio. Except for damage to her legs and some difficulty walking, she recovered. She married and had four children, one of whom died in infancy. After the fourth child was born, something went wrong and other muscles were severely weakened. Shira was confined to a wheelchair, with limited use of her arms and legs. Heavy doses of cortisone treatment made her overweight. Despite this, and perhaps because of this, she is an inspiration to others. She laughs and jokes and cares about others. To keep some of the mitzvos requires tremendous effort on Shira's part, but she makes that effort. In her *Yiddishkeit* she is uncompromising.

Gila lost the use of both legs in an accident. She was an incredibly beautiful girl, and even in a wheelchair she received admiring glances.

Gila had been a well-known dancer, and her accident put an end to her career. I looked at some of the pictures of her, taken before the accident, and she had been very lovely. However, after the accident she gained an inner beauty as well and was an inspiration to look at and talk to.

When Gila first came to me, not long after the accident, she kept comparing her present condition to the past and was extremely depressed. I suggested that she view her life in two stages. Before her accident she had been an attractive and admired dancer. That person had suffered a terrible accident and had, in essence died. She did not exist anymore. Now there was a new Gila who had a mission to fulfill. This Gila could not walk, but she had other talents.

Though her past was dead in some respects, we returned to it to search for undeveloped areas Gila could not work on.

"I used to like school at certain times, but most of the time I was bored and would daydream. I used to make up stories in my head to keep myself going. I invented all the characters, princes and princesses..."

Gila had never pursued any academic activity after leaving school, because her dancing had taken all her time. Now she began to study and found that this quenched a thirst she had not even known existed. She also began to write, using the imaginative ability she had developed as a child.

Now her life was taking off in a totally unanticipated direction. And she was enjoying every minute.

Disability is an opportunity to start a new life. Obviously there are increased challenges and hardships, but the sense of satisfaction in overcoming them is without measure.

Chapter 13

THE PSYCHOLOGY
OF THE JEW

I s there a particular Jewish psychology? Does the Jew differ from the non-Jew psychologically?

If a Jew is not complete without Torah, then there must be differences between a Jew who is keeping Torah and mitzvos and satisfying the deepest yearnings of his soul and the one who is not.

According to Rambam, man was originally created with a natural, inborn drive to do mitzvos. It was no different from his need for food, drink, or sleep. He found the performance of Hashem's commandments as gratifying as the pursuit of the other functions that are necessary if life is to be preserved. But when man met his first snake, the original and most destructive snake of all, he fell victim to temptation and changed. Even though the fulfillment of Hashem's commandments is just as essential to life and well-being as food, drink, and sleep, we are no longer driven by a compelling urge to comply with them. A special effort is now needed to perform the mitzvos.

To a psychologist these concepts present a profound challenge. There are two challenges Judaism places before a person. First, the fulfillment of Hashem's commandments is essential to the Jew even though there is no longer a conscious drive within him to fulfill them. Second, the Jew must expend a special effort to fulfill these commandments. In other words, although religious faith and practice are vitally essential to a Jew, this is not immediately apparent to him. He must make a special effort of will to come to this understanding.

This can be compared to someone who is seriously dehydrated. At this point he no longer feels thirsty and must make a conscious effort to drink. It has been said that Torah and mitzvos is for the Jewish soul what vitamins are for the body. They make up the essential building blocks of the Jewish soul. Yet we must make a conscious effort to keep the Torah.

I once conducted research on this subject to determine the effect of Torah and mitzvos on a Jew. I conducted a series of psychometric testing in Israel, comparing religious and nonreligious Jews regarding various personality factors.

It soon became obvious that a lack of *Yiddishkeit* caused a great deal of anxiety. The nonreligious Jew had a significantly higher degree of depression and anxiety. These factors stemmed from a sense of meaningless, of living without purpose. On the other hand, the nonreligious Jew tended to have less anxiety regarding material circumstances than did the religious group.

The nonreligious Jew also had a higher degree of covert depression and anxiety. This fundamental malaise may run too deep to be recognized on a conscious level. This accords with the Rambam's view that the Jew is not aware of his need for the spiritual.

Anxiety relating to interpersonal relationships was higher in the nonreligious Jew. Religious marriages were more stable, and there was a better adjustment for the religious newlywed on every level.

At the Forty-third Convention of the Orthopsychiatric Association held in San Francisco many years ago, Dr. Erich Fromm, in his opening address, made the following statement:

> In psychoanalytic terms, an individual's repressed unconscious feelings govern his behavior. That which is repressed today is the underlying anxiety, depression, loneliness, boredom, and pain about the meaninglessness of life. Freud's instinctual urges are no longer repressed. They belong to the present and are easily and cheaply reached.

Dr. David Perk, a South African psychiatrist, said, "The existentialist view that life is a meaningless exercise, conclusively confirmed by death, is more a symptom of a psychiatric disturbance than a philosophical insight."

I recently found out some very compelling research. In a sixteen-year (1970 to 1985) historical prospective study of mortality in eleven religious and eleven secular kibbutzim in Israel, the mortality rate in the secular kibbutzim was nearly twice that of the religious kibbutzim. The lower mortality rate in religious kibbutzim was consistent for all major causes of death.

Membership in a cohesive religious community promoted overall well-being and health. This ties in with the studies cited earlier which showed a lower incidence of heart disease among the religious Jewish population.

A strong social support system and an element of spirituality and religion seem to be the most consistent predictors of quality of life and possible survival among patients with advanced malignant disease.

An interesting insight comes from the Department of Occupational Therapy of the University of Southern California at Los Angeles. Ethnographic methods were used to study the occupations and routines of four young Orthodox Jewish couples living in Los Angeles. The data demonstrated the importance to the couples of fulfilling Divine commandments, which give structure and meaning to the mundane activities of daily living, such as eating, bathing, sleeping, and rising. Their study focused on observing the Sabbath, studying and praying, and keeping kosher. Religious Jewish life is time-bound and action-oriented. They noted that occupational therapists can benefit from understanding how religious Jews are able to invest spiritual significance in seemingly mundane routines.

Religious Jews are a special cultural group; their entire lives revolve around the teachings of the Torah. Their religious beliefs are reflected in all aspects of their lives, in both health and illness.

Conclusion

SNAKES AND LADDERS AGAIN

Let's look once again at our Snakes and Ladders board. We have met several snakes, gone on many trips, and witnessed people who have turned their snakes into ladders. We have seen that to turn a snake into a ladder we must be willing to change and be ready to work hard.

The game board of life never consists *only* of ladders. There will always be snakes, and when we conquer one, another one will emerge. This is our world. Until Mashiach comes, there will always be problems.

We have seen that through changing our thought patterns we can straighten our cognitive distortions. We can feel happy instead of feeling resentful, insecure, and unworthy. We can create an atmosphere of calm, whether within ourselves, our homes, or our community at large.

We can let go of the anger and the bitterness which erodes the soul and make peace with our inner selves.

All this takes constant, daily work. Feeling good is a discipline, but a discipline worth mastering.

BIBLIOGRAPHY

Alcoholics Anonymous. *Twelve Steps and Twelve Traditions*. 1953. Reprint, New York: AA World Services, 1993.

Allred, G. H. "Counseling in Parent-Child Relationships." In *Klesmer's Counseling in Marital and Sexual Problems*. Edited by R. F. Stahman and W. J. Hiebert. Baltimore: Williams and Wilkins Co., 1977.

Appel, K. E. "Religion." Ch. 89 in *The American Handbook of Psychiatry*. Edited by Silvano Arieti. New York: Basic Books Inc., 1959.

Attala, J. M. "Detecting Abuse against Women in the Home." *Home Care Provider*, vol. 1, no. 1 (January–February 1996): pp. 12–18.

Baily, Roy D. *Coping with Stress in Caring*. London: Blackwell Scientific Publications, 1985.

Bakker, R. H., P. P. Groenewegen, L. Jabaaij, W. Meijer, H. Sixma, and A. de Veer. " 'Burnout' among Dutch Midwives." *Midwifery* (Scotland), vol. 12, no. 4 (December 1996): pp. 174–181.

Beaton, R. D., S. A. Murphy, K. C. Pike, and W. Corneil. "Social Support and Network Conflict in Firefighters and Paramedics." *Western Journal of Nursing Research*, vol. 19, no. 3 (June 1997): pp. 297–313.

Benjamin, Barney. "Clinical Approaches to the Control of Stress." In *The Understanding and Treatment of Urban Stress*. Edited by B. Levinson. Johannesburg: Melton Publications, 1982.

Benjamin, Ruth V. "A Comparative Psychological Study of Religious and Non-religious Jews in Israel." Master's thesis, University of South Africa, Pretoria, 1972.

———. "Children and Divorce." *The Leech*, vol. 54, no. 1 (May 1984): pp. 8–15.

Berk, Michael. Personal communication. Department of Psychiatry, University of Witwatersrand Medical School, 1997.

Berne, Eric. *Games People Play*. New York: Penguin Books, 1964.

Bernhard, Rabbi Nachman M. "Premarital Counseling Session for Brides." Session held at the Oxford Synagogue Center, Johannesburg, South Africa, 1969.

Bocker, J., O. P. Tadmor, M. Gal, and Y. Z. Diamant. "The Prevalence of Adenomyosis and Endometriosis in an Ultra-religious Jewish Population." *Asia-Oceania Journal of Obstetrics and Gynecology* (Japan), vol. 20, no. 2 (June 1994): pp. 125–129.

Bourne, Edmund J. *The Anxiety and Phobia Workbook*. Oakland, Calif.: New Harbinger Publications Ltd., 1990.

Boyle, G. J., M. G. Borg, J. M. Falzon, A. J. Baglioni, Jr. "A Structural Model of the Dimensions of Teacher Stress." Part 1. *British Journal of Educational Psychology*, vol. 65 (March 1995): pp. 49–67.

Burke, R. J. "Stressful Events, Work-Family Conflict, Coping, Psychological Burnout, and Well-Being among Police Officers." *Psychological Reports*, vol. 75, no. 2 (October 1994): pp. 787–800.

Burns, David D. *Feeling Good: The New Mood Therapy*. New York: Signet Books, 1981.

———. *The Feeling Good Handbook*. New York: Plume, 1990.

Carmel, S., and S. M. Glick. "Compassionate-Empathic Physicians: Personality Traits and Social-Organizational Factors that Enhance or Inhibit This Behavior Pattern." *Social Science and Medicine* (England), vol. 43, no. 8 (October 1996): pp. 1,253–1,261.

Carrington, Patricia. Foreword to *Stress for Success*, by D. R. Morse and M. L. Furst. New York: Van Nostrand Reinhold Company, 1979.

Chan, D. W. and E. K. Hui. "Burnout and Coping among Chinese Secondary Schoolteachers in Hong Kong." Part 1. *British Journal of Educational Psychology*, vol. 65 (March 1995): pp. 15–25.

Creagan, E. T. "Attitude and Disposition: Do They Make a Difference in Cancer Survival?" *Mayo Clinic Proceedings*, vol. 72, no. 2 (February 1997): pp. 160–164.

Davidhizar, R. E., and R. Shearer. "Using Humor to Cope with Stress in Home Care." *Home Healthcare Nurse*, vol. 14, no. 10 (October 1996): pp. 825–830.

Dembo Y., I. Levin, and R. S. Siegler. "A Comparison of the Geometric Reasoning of Students Attending Israeli Ultra-Orthodox and Mainstream Schools." *Developmental Psychology*, vol. 33, no. 1 (January 1997): pp. 92–103.

Donin, Rabbi H. *To Raise a Jewish Child*. New York: Basic Books Inc., 1977.

Dougan, Barbara, Rene Dembo, Kate Lenahan, Refilwe Makapela, Jane Gama, and Driekie Moutinho. *Life Skills for Self-Development*. Johannesburg: National Council for Mental Health, 1986.

Drever, James. *A Dictionary of Psychology*. Great Britain: Penguin Books, 1952.

Dyer, Wayne. *Pulling Your Own Strings*. New York: Avon Publishers, 1978.

Edelwich, J., and A. Brodsky. *Burnout: Stages of Disillusionment in the Helping Professions*. New York: Human Science Press, 1980.

Fensterheim, Herbert, and Jean Bear. *Don't Say Yes When You Want to Say No*. London: Warner Books, 1975.

Fields, A. I., T. T. Cuerdon, C. O. Brasseux, P. R. Getson, A. E. Thompson, J. P. Orlowski, and S. J. Younger. "Physician Burnout in Pediatric Care Medicine." *Critical Care Medicine*, vol. 23, no. 8 (August 1995): pp. 1,425–1,429.

Flett, R., H. Biggs, and F. Alpass. "Job-Related Tension, Self-Esteem, and Psychological Distress in Rehabilitation Professionals." *International Journal of Rehabilitation Research*, vol. 18, no. 2 (June 1995): pp. 123–131.

Frank, G., C. S. Bernardo, S. Tropper, F. Noguchi, C. Lipman, B. Maulhardt, and L. Weitze. "Jewish Spirituality through Actions in Time: Daily Occupations of Young Orthodox Jewish Couples in Los Angeles." *American Journal of Occupational Therapy*, vol. 51, no. 3 (March 1997): pp. 199–206.

Frankl, Victor E. *Man's Search for Meaning*. Rev. ed. London: Hodder and Stroughton, 1964.

Fry, P. S. "Perfectionism, Humor, and Optimism as Moderators of Health Outcomes and Determinants of Coping Styles of Women Executives." *Genetic, Social, and General Psychological Monographs*, vol. 121, no. 2 (May 1995): pp. 211–245.

Gardener, H. *Developmental Psychology*. Boston: Little, Brown, 1978.

Gillis, L. S. *Guidelines in Psychiatry*. Capetown: David Philip Publisher Ltd., 1977.

Goldberg, R., R. W. Boss, L. Chan, J. Goldberg, W. K. Mallon, D. Moradzadeh, E. A. Goodman, and M. L. McConkie. "Burnout and Its Correlates in Emergency Physicians: Four Years' Experience with a Wellness Booth." *Academy of Emergency Medicine*, vol. 3, no. 12 (December 1996): pp. 1,156–1,164.

Goldbourt, U., S. Yaari, and J. H. Medalie. "Factors Predictive of Long-Term Coronary Heart Disease Mortality among 10,059 Male Israeli Civil Servants and Municipal Employees." A twenty-three-year mortality follow-up on the Israeli Ischemic Heart Disease Study. Parts 2–3. *Cardiology*, vol. 82 (1993): pp. 100–121.

Goldenson, Robert M. *Dictionary of Psychology and Psychiatry*. New York and London: Longman, 1984.

Harris, T. A. *I'm OK, You're OK*. London: Pan Books, 1973.

Healthnet (http://www.healthnet.ivi.com/en/bin/iatoc.bln?), August 18, 1997.

Heerwagen, J. H., J. G. Heubach, J. Montgomery, and W. C. Weimar. "Environmental Design, Work, and Well-Being: Managing Occupational Stress through Changes in the Workplace Environment." *American Association of Occupational Health Nurses Journal (AAOHN)*, vol. 43, no. 9 (September 1995): pp. 458–468.

Helps, S. "Experiences of Stress in Accident and Emergency Nurses."*Accident and Emergency Nursing*, vol. 5, no. 1 (January 1997): pp. 48–53.

Hiebert, W. J., and R. F. Stahmann. "Commonly Recurring Couple Interaction Patterns. In *Klesmer's Counseling in Marital and Sexual Problems*. Baltimore: Williams and Wilkins Co., 1977.

Horowitz, M. J. "Short-Term Therapeutic Interventions in Stress-Related Disorders." Ch. 8 in *Stress in Health and Disease*. Edited by Michael Zales. New York: Brunner/Mazel, 1985.

Houben, G. J., and F. J. Nijhuis. "The Role of Production Control in the Development of Burnout." *The Netherlands International Journal of Health Service*, vol. 26, no. 2 (1996): pp. 331–353.

Kark, J. D., R. Sinnreich, N. Goldberger, and Y. Friedlander. "Psychosocial Factors among Members of Religious and Secular Kibbutzim." *Israel Journal of Medical Sciences* (Israel), vol. 32, no. 3–4 (March–April 1996): pp. 185–194.

Kark, J. D., G. Shemi, Y. Friedlander, O. Martin, O. Manor, and S. H. Blondheim. "Does Religious Observance Promote Health?: Mortality in Secular versus Religious Kibbutzim in Israel." *American Journal of Public Health*, vol. 86, no. 3 (March 1996): pp. 341–346.

Kaslow, F. W. "Marital and Family Therapy." Ch. 30 in *Handbook and Marriage and the Family*. Edited by M. B. Sussman and S. K. Steinmetz. New York: Plenum Press, 1978.

Katz, Rabbi Avraham. *Designer World*. Gateshead, England: GJBS, 1994.

Kety, S. S. "Interactions between Stress and Genetic Processes." Ch. 4 in *Stress in Health and Disease*. Edited by Michael Zales. New York: Brunner/Mazel, 1985.

Knoop, R. "Relieving Stress through Value-Rich Work." *Journal of Social Psychology*, vol. 134, no. 6 (1994): pp. 829–836.

Levinson, B. "Stress and the Doctor." In *The Understanding and Treatment of Urban Stress*. Johannesburg: Melton Publications, 1982.

Levinson, H. *Executive Stress*. New York: Harper and Row Publications, 1964.

Magnusson, A. E., D. K. Nias, and P. D. White. "Is Perfectionism Associated with Fatigue?" *Journal of Psychosomatic Research*, vol. 41, no. 4 (October 1996): pp. 377–383.

McLean, A. A. "The Corporate Environment and Stress." Ch. 6 in *Stress in Health and Disease*. Edited by Michael Zales. New York: Brunner/Mazel, 1985.

Modigh, K., and C. Nordlund. "Anxiety with Panic Attacks: A Treatment Program." *Psychiatric Insight*, vol. 3, no. 1 (1986): pp. 3–9.

Morse, D. R., and M. Furst. *Stress for Success*. New York: Van Nostrand Reinhold Company, 1979.

Muldary, Thomas W. *Burnout and Health Professionals: Manifestations and Management*. Norwalk, Conn.: Appelton-Century-Crofts, 1983.

Orth-Gomer, K., V. Moser, M. Blom, S. P. Wamala, and Schenck-Gustafsson. "Survey of Stress in Women: Heart Disease in Stockholm Women Is Caused by Both Family- and Work-Related Stress." *Lakartidningen* (Sweden), vol. 94, no. 8 (February 19, 1997), pp. 632, 635–638.

Otten, R. "The Practical Management of Stress." In *The Understanding and Treatment of Urban Stress*. Edited by B. Levinson. Johannesburg: Melton Publications, 1982.

Perk, Dr. David. *Man's Quest for Meaning, Faith, and Identity*. Johannesburg: Ageas Press, 1975.

Pichot, D., and J. Hassan. "Masked Depression and Depressive Equivalents." In *Masked Depression*. Edited by P. Keilholtz. Bern, Switzerland: Hans Huber Publisher, 1973.

Pretorius, T. B. "Using the Maslach Burnout Inventory to Assess Educators' Burnout at a University in South Africa." *Psychological Reports*, vol. 75, no. 2 (October 1994): pp. 771–777.

Ramirez, A. J., J. Graham, M. A. Richards, A. Cull, W. M. Gregory, M. S. Leaning, D. C.. Snashall, and A. R. Timothy. "Burnout and Psychiatric Disorder among Cancer Clinicians." *British Journal of Cancer*, vol. 71, no. 6 (June 1995): pp. 1,263–1,269.

Rosenman, R. H., and M. A. Chesney. "Type A Behavior Pattern: Its Relationship to Coronary Heart Disease and Its Modifications by Behavioral and Pharmacological Approaches." Ch. 9 in *Stress in Health and Disease*. Edited by Michael Zales. New York: Burnner/Mazel, 1985.

Rubin, T. *Dr. Rubin, Please Make Me Happy*. Bantam Books, 1974.

Satir, V. *Conjoint Family Therapy*. Palo Alto, Calif.: Science and Behavior Books Inc., 1967.

Schlebusch, L., A. J. Lasich, and W. K. Wessels. "Exacerbation of Spontaneous Panic Attacks." *Psychothreapeia* (South Africa), no. 43 (May/June 1986): pp. 5–7.

Schneerson, Rabbi Y. Y. *Likkutei Dibburim*. Translated by Uri Kaploun. New York: Kehot Publications Society, 1987.

Selye, H. "Stress and a Holistic View of Health for the Nursing Profession." In *Living with Stress and Promoting Well-Being*. Edited by K. Claus and J. Bailey. St. Louis: C. V. Mosby, 1980.

Snyder, J., and B. Sommer. "Special Considerations for Orthodox Jewish

Patients in the Emergency Department." *Journal of Emergency Nursing*, vol. 21, no. 6 (December 1995): pp. 569–570.

Steen, E., A. C. Naess, and P. A. Steen. "Paramedics Organizational Culture and Their Care for Relatives of Cardiac Arrest Victims." *Resuscitation* (Norway), vol. 34, no. 1 (February 1997): pp. 57–63.

Stein, M., and S. J. Schleifer. "Frontiers of Stress Research: Stress and Immunity." Ch. 3 in *Stress in Health and Disease*. Edited by Michael Zales. New York: Brunner/Mazel, 1985.

Stein, Edward V. *Guilt Theory and Therapy*. Philadelphia: Westminster Press, 1968.

Tehune, W. B. *Emotional Problems and What You Can Do About Them*. New York: William Morrow and Co., 1961.

Trower, Peter, Andrew Casey, and Windy Dryden. *Cognitive Behavioral Counseling in Action*. London: Sage Publications, 1988.

Tsenova, V., T. Tatozov, T. S. Antonova, and M. Tsvetkova. "The Prevalance of the Burnout Syndrome in the Personnel of Children's Institutions." *Probl Khig* (Bulgaria), vol. 20 (1995): pp. 90–100.

Twerski, Abraham J. *Generation to Generation*. New York: Tradition Press, 1985.

———. *Like Yourself and Others Will Too*. New York: Prentice Hall Press, 1986.

Vardi, G., B. Modan, R. Golan, I. Novikov, and R. Shafir. "Orhtodox Jews Have a Lower Incidence of Malignant Melanoma." A note on the potentially protective role of traditional clothing. *International Journal of Cancer*, vol. 53, no. 5 (March 12, 1993): pp. 771–773.

Veninga, R. L. and J. P. Spradley. *The Work Stress Connection: How to Cope with Job Burnout*. Boston: Little, Brown, 1981.

Walton and Fazarkerley Hospitals, Liverpool, Department of Occupational Therapy. *You and Your Anxiety*.

Walters, V., R. Lenton, S. French, J. Eyles, J. Mayr, and B. Newbold. "Paid Work, Unpaid Work, and Social Support: A Study of the Health of Male and Female Nurses." *Social Science and Medicine*, vol. 43, no. 11 (December 1996): pp. 1,627–1,636.

Winokur, George. *Depression: The Facts*. Great Britain: Oxford University Press, 1981.

Zales, Michael, ed. *Stress in Health and Disease*. A product of the 21st Annual Meeting of the American College of Psychiatrists, held in 1984 in Coronado, Calif. New York: Brunner/Mazel, 1985.

Zevin, Y. *A Treasury of Chassidic Tales.* New York: Mesorah Publications Ltd., 1980.